T0265775

Real Coaches' Praise for *Coach Builder*

"There are many books that discuss the framework of a coaching session. However, if you don't have a repeatable process to obtain and retain clients, there is no one for you to coach. *Coach Builder* gives its readers a very clear and concise road map for the launch and growth of a solo coaching business and critical action items necessary in scaling toward a seven-figure coaching agency."   —DAVID PATTERSON, business coach since 2012

"Most of the business coaching books and programs focus on mindset and have few practical tools to help you actually get your business off the ground. When I was preparing to launch my coaching business, I spent hundreds of dollars on books and thousands on programs that didn't give me anywhere near the practical tools and momentum found in this book. If you're serious about starting a coaching business, this is the primary book for your shelf. Read it, implement the eight steps, and watch your business soar."   —SETH WINTERHALTER, business coach since 2022

"I've come to expect practical insights and actionable advice in any offering from Donald Miller. This book takes it to a new level. This is a strategic outline for how to be done with winging-it-and-wondering, as well as an applicable plan of action for anyone who has a deep desire to coach others but has no real idea how to build a coaching business."   —ERIC FLETCHER, business coach since 2017

"Don's eight-step plan is spot on!! A new coach could take this book and work through these steps to launch and grow a successful coaching practice. I especially took Step Seven to heart—Build or Join a Coaching Community. Don't skip this chapter or minimize the importance of building a community you can turn to for support and inspiration."   —SUSAN TRUMPLER, business coach since 2013

"In a time when small business owners are facing more challenges and drastic changes in the marketplace than ever before, this book empowers business coaches with a simple yet strategic approach to build their own business so they can in turn support the small businesses that need their help. Whether experienced or new, it's clear and easy to understand. Don Miller breaks down the potential complexity of lead generation and growth into simple steps and straightforward terms—no 'business jargon.' It's a wonderful resource recommended to me by a business professional I trust and respect. Any business coach will benefit from reading this book—especially those at the beginning of growing their business—and will bring a lot more to the table with the knowledge and action steps it provides." —MARY CZARNECKI, business coach since 2016

"As the coaching industry (life, health, business, etc.) grows, the need for a book like *Coach Builder* becomes even more necessary. Like any entrepreneur launching a business, just because you are good at what you do doesn't translate into knowing how to build your coaching business. *Coach Builder* shares simple, practical steps that will help any kind of coach successfully remove the guesswork about how to build their coaching business." —KENNY CAMP, business coach since 2018

"After helping hundreds of people launch and grow a business, I know that having a step-by-step approach to growing your business is a critical piece of your business success story. Don provides you with the eight critical steps that will allow you to quickly get your business to the next level in a way that's easy to follow and even easier to implement. You will be shocked at the speed and the impact it has on your business! Implement what Don tells you, and watch your business soar!" —JESSICA MILLER, business coach since 2016

"The field of coaching can be rife with philosophical approaches and unclear frameworks for how to best serve clients. *Coach Builder* gives a step-by-step approach for creating a business that will help you take that leap and leave your W2. You'll learn how to strategically and practically put systems in place to generate leads and revenue that will launch, grow, and scale your business in the way you want. It won't be easy, but it will be straightforward if you follow Don's guidance—after several years as a certified coach, I can say that this process works!"

—JASON DAILY,
business coach since 2011

COACH BUILDER

**HOW TO TURN YOUR EXPERTISE INTO A
PROFITABLE COACHING CAREER**

DONALD MILLER

HarperCollins
LEADERSHIP

An Imprint of HarperCollins

ISBN 978-1-4002-2808-9 (eBook)
ISBN 978-1-4002-2696-2 (HC)
ISBN 978-1-4002-4899-5 (ITPE)

Library of Congress Control Number: 2023948649

Printed in the United States of America
23 24 25 26 27 LBC 5 4 3 2 1

Contents

Author's Note

Coach Builder is written for anybody who has succeeded in business and wants to leverage their experience to start or grow a profitable consulting career.

The examples in this book are mostly related to business coaching but the steps to build a coaching business will work for a business coach, a life coach, a financial advisor, a gardening consultant, a parenting coach, a real estate agent, or in any other field of interest. If you want to coach but not in business, simply apply the steps to your field of expertise.

Your experience and the knowledge you've accumulated are more valuable than you think. They can be turned into a coaching business, but only if you follow the steps in this book. Here's to your success.

The Eight Steps That Will Grow Your Coaching Business

ave you ever wished you could make money meeting with people and changing their lives forever? Have you accomplished enough in your career that you want to share your experience with others?

If that's true for you, what you're pining for is a career as a coach.

In fact, if you're reading this book, you're likely already a business coach. You may not be one by title just yet, but you're doing the thing coaches do: helping business owners succeed in their life and work.

Business leaders need good coaches. The quality of people's lives and the strength of our economies depend upon coaches who pass along instruction and encouragement. In fact, if a business owner had to choose between getting a master's in business from a prestigious university or hiring a coach, I'd counsel them to hire the coach. A coach has the power to help their client make millions—and not only that, to stay sane while doing so. It is important that you succeed as a coach because it's important that your clients succeed in their careers.

Because this book is written as a playbook, it is going to be practical. Every step will give you an action you can take to create or grow your coaching business. Plenty of coaches have gone before you and made it work. I promise, you can build a profitable coaching business, too.

HOW CAN YOU BUILD A PROFITABLE COACHING BUSINESS?

Many coaches launch their coaching business after experiencing a level of success in a career or a business of their own. What they realize after they launch their coaching business is that in their previous career they did not develop the full set of skills necessary to wear all of the hats required to build a successful coaching business. They never had to create a website, manage a pipeline of potential clients, create products for those clients, or sell and upsell those products, all of which are necessary to grow a coaching business.

This book is designed to help you close this knowledge gap and build a coaching business you can be proud of.

Whether you're just starting out in coaching or have been coaching for years, the eight steps that follow will help you build a coaching business from the ground up.

So what are the eight steps? I will summarize the steps here, but keep reading. I share the real secrets in the chapters to come.

STEP ONE:
Create a Menu of Products You Can Sell to Clients
Before we think about attracting clients, let's stop and think about what we are going to sell them. In order to grow a coaching

business, or any business for that matter, you need a defined list of products. Your coaching products can span from a simple assessment to workshops, masterminds, and even retreats. Each of your products should be easy to understand, deliver extreme value, and be offered at a premium price. Designing products you can offer for a premium price is the only way you will be able to build wealth while being fully present with your clients. When I take you through step one, I'll show you several kinds of coaching products you can create and sell to your clients.

STEP TWO:
Create and Manage a Potential Client List
Most coaches are surrounded by potential clients but are unaware that the people they're interacting with would pay a premium for their services. Creating and managing a robust list of potential clients and communicating with those clients in a way that earns trust is the fastest way to grow your coaching business. When I walk you through step two I will introduce you to a simple and effective system you can use to organize your client pipeline, gain your clients' trust, and convert leads into paying customers.

STEP THREE:
Get Your Website (Sales Pitch) Right
The number of coaches who do not create or maintain an effective website is frightening. Even if we don't want or need to formally announce our services, having an effective website is necessary if we are going to practice what we preach. Every business needs to create an elevator pitch and menu of services in the form of a landing page. Your website can be an example of how to effectively communicate a solid offer to potential clients and as

such provide an example for your clients to follow. To provide a good example to your clients, your pitch must be attractive, clear, and designed to close sales. When I walk you through step three I will show you the critical parts of an effective sales pitch in the form of a coaching website.

STEP FOUR:
Learn to Write Great Emails That Close the Deal

The most effective way to build trust with potential clients is to provide value over time. And a proven way to provide value over time (without overextending yourself) is to follow up with leads using an automated email system. When you reach out to potential clients with at least twelve helpful emails that include tips, tools, and strategies they can use to grow their businesses, you earn the trust of those clients and increase the chance they will engage in one or more of your coaching products. When we get to step four, I'll show you an array of effective emails that will convert potential clients into paying customers.

STEP FIVE:
Map Out Your Client Journey by Creating a Marketing and Product Ladder

Deciding to work with a coach will require baby steps on the part of your clients. They will need to get to know you and trust you in order to invest and go on to invest even more. If you create a marketing ladder, you can slowly earn their trust, and if you create a product ladder, you will have a way for those who get results to invest more and more in your services. When you create these two ladders you will always know where a client is at on their journey, and you will better be able to help them take the next step.

STEP SIX:

Establish Realistic Goals and Accomplish Those Goals
We all know that to succeed we've got to set goals and then accomplish those goals. But what goals should a business coach pursue and how ambitious should those goals be? Now that we have products to sell and a list of clients who can buy them, it's time to set some realistic goals. Making a list of goals in a few specific categories will motivate you to build the dependable coaching business of your dreams. When we get to step six I'll share the necessary goal-setting categories with you and help you make a plan to achieve those goals.

STEP SEVEN:

Build or Join a Coaching Community That Will Help You Grow Yourself and Your Business
If you want to be a great coach, surround yourself with great coaches. There's no reason to build your coaching business in a vacuum. Plenty of wisdom about building a coaching business is out there—all you have to do is join or start a coaching community. Step seven involves being in community with other coaches. If you don't have that kind of community, I'll show you how easy it is to build one.

STEP EIGHT:

Master the Soft Skills of Coaching
The Coach Builder Playbook can't help a person grow a coaching business if they aren't good with people. When people sign up for your coaching, they aren't trusting your playbooks or frameworks; they're trusting you. But what sort of soft skills does a coach need to have in order to generate trust? When we get to

step eight I will help you develop a personal list of "rules" you can live by that make you the sort of coach paying clients love to spend time with.

USE BEST PRACTICES TO BUILD YOUR COACHING BUSINESS

When you take the eight steps I've listed above, you should be able to grow a strong, six-figure coaching business in under a year and then double the size of that business within the following eighteen months. If you want to take it even further, I've included a playbook at the end of this book to take your coaching business into seven figures and beyond.

The world does not need another book about the philosophy of coaching. Those books have their place but let's not get lost in the macro. I want you to be able to put this book down, even after a short reading session, and create something that grows your business. And I want you to be able to do that over and over and over until you have transformed your entire coaching business into the sort of life-transforming machine that affords you your dream job working with your dream clients.

To make this book useful, I've included specific examples and templates you can use immediately. These templates have been tested by the hundreds of coaches I've worked with over the years and they have proven to be very effective.

What follows are what I have found over time to be the best practices in lead generation, marketing, networking, product creation, and product delivery that you can use immediately.

Let's get started with step one.

STEP ONE

Create a Menu of Products You Can Sell to Clients

If you're just starting out as a coach, you're probably wondering where, how, and when your first dollars are going to come in. If you are not asking yourself these questions, you should be. There are no more important concerns to have when running a business than how you're going to bring cash into the business, how you're going to *keep* cash coming into the business, and how you're going to change people's lives in a way that is consistent and sustainable. After all, your coaching business will not survive unless you're generating profitable revenue.

To grow your coaching business you will need to exchange value for dollars and you will need to do it often.

The fastest way to bring in cash is to have a menu of products you're able to sell that offer clear value and are sold at a stated price.

My friend Brek spent years as a pastor, giving free counsel and advice to anybody who attended his church. When he retired, he decided to leverage his experience counseling and developing spiritual leaders into the business world. As he made the transition, he told me how nervous he was to charge money for something people had been getting from him for free, for decades. Knowing that creating a menu of products was important, though, he put together a life-planning workshop and charged a fixed rate to take a leadership team from a small business through the process. After the workshop, the owner of the company asked if Brek could meet individually with each of his leaders for the rest of the year. Brek then created another one-on-one coaching product, attached a price to it, and sold it to the business owner. Now Brek has a life-planning workshop along with a series of follow-up one-on-ones that help his clients achieve work-life balance and accomplish their personal and professional goals.

What I loved most about hearing Brek's story wasn't just that his coaching business was changing lives, but that Brek was being transformed himself. As a pastor, he had not been charging directly for his incredible wisdom, causing him to believe it wasn't worth much, but when he discovered he could package his wisdom up, place a premium price tag on it, and exchange that value for money, he began to fully understand his own worth as a coach and mentor.

The reason so many coaching businesses struggle is because they only offer advice in a retainer format. Why? Because they haven't broken down their expertise into easily relatable products that offer clear value. For $500 you can meet with a coach like this a couple times per month and ask questions. The truth is, though, you never really know what you're getting. It almost feels like you're paying to have a friend.

The fact that this kind of simple, skinny product offering sometimes works to grow a coaching business is a miracle, or more accurately, proof that human beings are desperate for any kind of advice they can get.

I'm sure your advice is valuable and a certain intangible value gets exchanged every time you meet with a client. However, if your offering was more clear, you'd attract more clients and those clients would pay even more for the value you offer. And in the process, you will be transformed into an expert who fully believes in themselves and the value that they offer.

The problem with a vague offer such as retainer coaching is that it's difficult for the client to understand the value they are getting. Offering "business advice" on a retainer is akin to a restaurant that advertises "food items." They'd sell a lot more food if they advertised something more specific, like a cheese-burger or fried chicken or the best pizza in town.

Getting specific about what you offer will grow your coaching business faster than pushing the vague offering of "coaching."

A MENU OF COACHING
PRODUCTS IS PARAMOUNT

Creating a menu of products is important in any kind of coaching, not just business coaching.

My friend Nicole Burke started a garden in her backyard. Even though she had no experience as a gardener, she became so obsessed with the garden that she began talking to friends about how much lettuce her simple kitchen garden was producing and, of course, her friends had questions. The truth is, Nicole never felt like she knew that much about gardening. She was just good at it. Regardless, she began to visit her friends' houses giving them advice about where to place their gardens, which vegetables to plant in which seasons, and how to maintain their gardens once they were producing. All of this, again, was offered for free. That is until she got a tuition bill for one of her kids' schools. Nicole realized she was going to have to get a job. Instead of getting a job, though, she decided to keep consulting with friends and created a product, a $25-per-hour consulting fee to help people build a kitchen garden.

As you can imagine, her consulting became popular but it wasn't paying enough to cover her bills. She realized pretty quickly that she needed to charge more. She raised her price to $100 per hour and added raised flower beds, beds she built herself from wood she bought at Home Depot. Her clients couldn't get enough. She added trellises and arches to her menu of products and her clients bought them up.

Her business really started to grow when, having realized the business could not scale beyond herself, she began to certify people to coach others to create a kitchen garden. Today, Nicole runs a seven-figure garden consulting business called Gardenary and is aiming to have her own television show. She's written two books about starting a kitchen garden and she's constantly being featured in the media. She started as a hobbyist and has now been transformed into a true expert, coach, and thought leader in her space.

How did it all start for Nicole? It started with a passion that turned into a menu of products. Then she had the guts to charge for those products. That is how your coaching business will start, too.

When growing a coaching business, you should have a menu of products clients can choose from. Each product on that menu should declare tangible value. If you create this kind of menu, customers will be drawn to your coaching. Why? Because nobody wants to pull out their debit card and buy a patch of fog, and if you only offer "coaching advice" for a retainer, you're asking people to buy a patch of confusing fog.

Creating a menu of products is a critical and important step you can take in growing a coaching business.

In fact, knowing what products you are going to sell isn't only the first step in starting or growing a coaching business; it's the first step in growing any kind of business. Nobody can grow a business if they don't know what they're going to sell.

You will be much more successful (and confident) if you are specific about what you offer and how each item you offer will make your client a return on their investment. In other words, if you want to succeed as a business coach, you need to define each of your services as a specific item available for a specific price.

WHAT SORT OF COACHING PRODUCTS SHOULD YOU SELL?

What will your menu of products look like? Don't overthink it. If you're starting a consulting business, package together a group of hours that you will spend helping your clients solve a specific problem. For instance, if you have an expertise in global supply chains, you could create a consulting product called the "China Transition Analysis" in which you offer forty hours to analyze your clients' current supply chain and give them a report on what they could realistically source outside China. A product like this is going to be much more attractive than the offer of a black-box investment in which you offer to "look into it."

Here are several examples of products you could offer, for instance, if you were starting out as a small business coach:

- **Small Business Optimization Program:** Six months to one year of bimonthly coaching to overhaul your clients' entire small business operation.

- **Management and Operations Overhaul:** Six months of fractional COO services that will optimize your clients' management and operations.

- **The How to Close Big Sales Workshop:** One-day sales training for your clients' sales teams.

- **Double Your Sales Transformation Program:** Six months of ongoing sales coaching with your clients' entire sales team, helping them close larger sales, faster.

- **Product Profitability Audit:** A one-day consultation in which you meet with clients to rank their products from most to least profitable and then ideate around new product ideas and how they can deliver a more profitable product offering.

- **Leadership Alignment Workshop:** One-day leadership workshop to help your clients create their mission statement and guiding principles.

- **Weekly One-on-One "Double Your Revenue" Coaching:** A weekly coaching retainer that takes clients through a comprehensive curriculum designed to help them double their current revenue.

- **Elite Partners Mastermind:** One-year, elite mastermind of business owners only offered to your top-tier clients.

There are many more product ideas, of course, but this list will give you an idea of the products many coaches use to increase both the value they offer and the revenue they receive.

Again, when you create a menu of products to choose from, customers are more likely to place orders because you've made it easier for them to understand what they are getting in exchange for their dollars.

After creating a menu of products, you are going to stand out. Your coach offerings are going to be clear and, as such, will be understood and attractive to potential clients.

WHAT ARE BUSINESS OWNERS WILLING TO PAY FOR?

When deciding what to include in your menu of products, consider first what people are willing to pay for. As it relates to business, people are willing to invest in something that will get them a financial return on their investment. In other words, they are willing to invest money in order to get more money in return.

If you are coaching outside the business world, people are willing to pay to save time, to save frustration, to connect with others, to advance in their career, to give a good speech, to figure out how to help their newborn sleep on a schedule, to restore an old car, to learn a foreign language, to manage all those dating apps and find true love, to write their first book, and on and on. I once paid a friend (who wasn't even a coach although he should be) to help me create a new wardrobe because I was starting to do more videos on social media.

Our job as coaches, then, is to create products that offer tangible value. As business coaches, we can offer more than just financial value. We can offer peace of mind, higher morale among our clients' teams, community, more trusting relationships, and even networking opportunities.

Identifying what is frustrating to our clients and then helping them solve those frustrations is fundamental to our success as coaches.

Here's a great exercise: Take out a sheet of paper and write down all the problems your perfect client has as they relate to your field of expertise. What bothers them? Where are they wasting money? What are they afraid of? What are they insecure about? What is causing them physical pain? What is costing them emotional pain?

Now, on the other side of that sheet of paper, come up with products you can sell that solve those specific problems. You may not have a product for each pain point, or you may have a product or two that solves multiple problems, but the point of the exercise is to help us all understand that people spend money to solve problems, and if there are people who need your expertise in order to solve a specific problem, you've got a product opportunity.

As it relates to business coaching, what problems are business leaders encountering that you could help solve? Do small business owners feel like their entire team is unfocused, wasting thousands of dollars in payroll expense? Yes, therefore your fractional COO product will align their team around economic objectives that drive revenue, profit, and growth, transforming payroll from a loss into a strategic investment.

Is the sales team failing to close big sales and are the lead times too long? If so, your one-day sales training combined with six months of coaching will energize the sales team and equip them to close larger sales, faster. The result? Your clients' sales teams could actually double their sales.

When each coaching product you create correlates with an opportunity for your client to solve a problem, potential clients will be more likely to make a purchase.

As it relates to business coaching, you're going to want to make your client money. Small businesses eat cash and they eat a lot of cash. Often, even if a small business is making millions in revenue, their earnings are dismal. Make sure, then, that some or most of your products connect directly with your clients' bottom line.

HOW CAN YOU HELP A SMALL
BUSINESS OWNER MAKE MONEY?

If you're a business coach, don't be intimidated by the responsibility to help your client make money. You may not be able to act as a fractional COO yet and you may not be able to teach a sales workshop yet, but the truth is you are already good at something that will help your clients make money, and whatever you are good at could be turned into a product.

If you're excellent at marketing and messaging, one of your products could be a six-month marketing overhaul. If you are excellent at tax strategy, you could lead with a tax strategy playbook.

What is it that you're good at? If you are terrific at goal setting and accountability, start a six-month mastermind in which every member establishes their goals and works with you to achieve them within 180 days. Call that small group the "Goal Accelerator Program" and charge $5,000 per member. Then, when the experience is over, offer to take each of your clients' entire teams through the process. If you become known as the coach who helps people achieve their goals, especially their financial goals, you will be busy, I promise.

HOW CAN YOU MAKE A FAST, GUARANTEED INCOME IF YOU ARE JUST STARTING OUT IN COACHING?

If you are just starting out in coaching, I recommend creating one flagship product and promoting it almost exclusively (while building out the rest of your product menu) during your first year. When you create your flagship product, though, remember two things:

1. Offer extreme value to your clients.

2. Don't let the product monopolize all of your time. You need to reserve enough time to strategize and execute the growth of the rest of your coaching business.

One great idea that fits both of these characteristics is to launch a flagship small group.

The key to a successful flagship small group is to offer a specific deliverable within a precise timeline. For instance, you can offer a challenge to increase revenue by 25 percent over the course of six months. You will do this by helping each person overhaul their marketing, sales, and product optimization. Those three things, if executed well, should help your clients achieve more revenue.

The benefit of offering a specific deliverable through your flagship small group is that clients know what they're going to get and the small group doesn't feel too much like a black-box investment. And the benefits of having a set timeline are that you can start a new group every six months, and when it's done, you can invite clients into the rest of your menu of products as a natural next step.

Not only that, but by creating a low-cost small group as your first-year flagship product, you can batch your coaching to impact five, ten, or even more clients all at the same time.

If you're not a business coach, a small group that teaches potty training, dog obedience, keynote presentation skills, and more are all possible. In fact, while I coach coaches for a living, one of my favorite pastimes (and revenue streams) is a mastermind I teach that helps people write their first book. It's great fun and I fully believe the group gets more out of it because they learn as much from each other as they do from me.

Again, if you're just getting started as a coach, hosting a six-month small group will help you get a fast, lucrative start to your coaching business without eating up the time you will also need to build your potential client list and your subsequent marketing plan.

In fact, if you wanted, you could actually host a small group before you quit your existing day job—that is if your current work situation allows. There is nothing like having a revenue stream coming in before you take the leap to ease the burden of getting started.

USE YOUR FLAGSHIP PRODUCT TO CREATE A BASE-LEVEL REVENUE FOUNDATION FOR YOUR COACHING BUSINESS

If you're worried about how you're going to make money as a coach, you can start brainstorming the menu of products you will offer today. As you create your menu of products, you will feel a sense of optimism because you will start to understand the tangible value you are able to offer. Not only this, but creating a menu of products allows you to understand how many of each product you will need to sell in order to pay your bills and build wealth. Then, you can execute a plan to sell those products and achieve the freedom you've been dreaming about.

For example, here's how the money might work for you as a small business coach wanting to start or grow your coaching practice:

Before you quit your day job, you open up registrations for your flagship small group. If you are able to charge $5,000 per client and work with ten clients, you've got your first $50,000. Getting ten people to sign up is no easy challenge, but later in this chapter I will show you how to do that. Regardless, a $50,000 start is a decent foundation on which you can build.

How much time will operating this small group take? Not as much as you think. Your task list to host a small group is fairly simple. You will need to create a basic timeline for the group, including a start and stop date, a rough curriculum to follow that will help the members of your small group achieve success, and a lengthy checklist of all the things your clients need to do to see results. The lengthy checklist is key because it will allow you to cover everything on the checklist, and if they don't follow through, the checklist will reveal they didn't do the work and so should not expect a return on their investment.

Your first small group will take the most time, but once you've created the material, feel good about the timeline, and know what to focus on to help your clients get the best results, all you need to do is repeat the process every six months.

You might be wondering how your clients can get such great value by being in a small group in which you only interact with them for an hour each week. Remember this: The value isn't only coming from you. Entrepreneurs and small business owners don't get to talk to each other very often, and when they do, they learn a great deal. Your job as the coach is to facilitate a conversation, help your clients learn, teach them frameworks they can use to optimize their businesses, and hold them accountable to reach their goals. The group members themselves will continue to provide even more value to one another because you've curated the community and brought them together.

In fact, if you find that you are extroverted and love people, an entire business model can be created that exclusively offers community to business executives. My friend Bob Johnston has created a community exclusively for executives that has attracted hundreds of members and thousands of attendees. Bob hosts an online community, regional dinners that include speakers, an awards banquet, a podcast, and an inspirational on-demand video series. Bob's community is called Executive Council and has scaled well past seven figures in revenue.

The point is that a flagship small group is a great way to get your coaching business started and an even better way to create a revenue foundation to work from. On top of this, it serves as a base-level community and attendees can be invited to advance further into your menu of coaching products.

If starting a flagship small group sounds good to you, the next challenge will be to generate leads for potential small group clients. Let's tackle that challenge now.

COACH'S STORY

When I started my coaching business, I struggled to tell people how I could help them and close sales. I often felt like the vultures in *The Jungle Book* . . .

Buzzie: Hey, Flaps, what we gonna do?
Flaps: I don't know. What you wanna do?

Then, I'd spend hours trying to put together a proposal, and finally hit *send*—stressed and discouraged.

Clients carry tons of stuff on their shoulders all day. When they showed up looking for help, I needed to have a clear path for them.

After organizing my main offer, my one-off paid call (Jake on Demand), doing free keynotes, and setting up a paid call where I answered questions about their free assessment, I was able to reach more ideal clients and let them "sample" my coaching.

Then, more often than not, they would accept an offer. By organizing these offers into pathways and having them ready, I could simply present a clear path to a prospect and ask how soon they'd like to start. Then, I can return to the same clients offering them a deeper dive or a chance to the next level of growth.

—JAKE BROWN,
business coach since 2021

OFFER A ONETIME COACHING CALL THAT DELIVERS VALUE AND THEN INVITE THOSE CLIENTS TO JOIN YOUR NEXT SMALL GROUP

Few clients will pay you thousands for your coaching services before they've experienced the kind of value you offer. However, more clients will sign up for your flagship small group and then your retainer consulting if you first engage them in an initial, onetime coaching call that demonstrates your worth as a coach.

You've likely heard of sales funnels—that is, lead generators and subsequent emails that convert lookers into buyers—but have you ever thought about a product funnel? A product funnel consists of entry-level products that lead to more and more valuable products as the customer further experiences your offer.

I recently sat down with a small business coach who earns more than $600,000 per year through his small groups, one-on-one consulting, and workshops. Most of his income is generated in monthly retainer fees for a hybrid model of masterminds and one-on-one coaching.

"How did you get it all going?" I asked.

He said the secret was to invite clients to a free, sixty-minute consulting call, deliver significant value, and then invite them into a six-month coaching engagement. From there, he was able to introduce them to his fractional COO services as well as provide coaches for his clients' leadership team.

For most clients, your flagship small group will be enough of an introductory offer. However, if you're having trouble selling your flagship small group, create an even easier product to say yes to and then invite them into your small group. This product should be an easily affordable (or free), onetime interaction that, again, delivers extreme value.

The kind of onetime engagement I'm talking about should have three characteristics:

1. It should be less than ninety minutes long. The idea is to give your client a taste of the value they could be getting weekly or bimonthly if they joined your small group.

2. It should reveal and address the problems they are experiencing in their business so the client has clarity about why they need a coach.

3. It should have a name and a fixed price. We recommend charging anything from $0 to $495 for the initial session. You don't have to charge if you don't want to, but do remember that people value what they pay for and devalue what they don't pay for. Even if your introductory call is free, make sure

you charge for the very next coaching product they buy from you.

Examples of Paid Lead-Generating Products That Could Work for You

The One-Page Hiring Plan: Spend ninety minutes with a client to help them assess their current org chart and design a growth plan defining what their next five hires should be.

The Mission Statement Overhaul: Spend ninety minutes with a client helping them understand why their current mission statement is useless and show them how to create one that actually aligns a team and drives financial objectives.

The Perfect Presentation Outline: Spend ninety minutes with a client showing them the perfect presentation outline. You can even help them outline their next presentation so they can give the best possible keynote.

The Small Business Cash Flow Playbook: Spend ninety minutes with a client showing them how to manage money for their small business. You can introduce them to high-level concepts about how to put themselves on a salary, put money away for taxes, and move profit away from the company so it is protected.

The Hiring an Employee Protocol: Spend ninety minutes helping your client understand how to find, interview, and onboard a new team member.

The Firing an Employee Protocol: Spend ninety minutes helping your client understand the right way to fire an employee by walking through a checklist and then role-playing the firing conversation with them.

The Product Price Formula: Spend ninety minutes walking your clients through a formula helping them determine what to charge for their products and then help them assess their current prices to see if they are optimized for demand and profit.

The Marketing and Messaging Review: Spend ninety minutes with a client assessing the effectiveness of their website and marketing by walking them through a checklist of "must haves" in a small business marketing plan.

The "Perfect Week" Planning Tool: Spend ninety minutes helping your client plan their perfectly productive week and then coach them on how to structure their time to duplicate that week as often as possible.

The Tax Exposure Checklist: Spend ninety minutes with a client going through a list of tax strategies any small business should be using to lessen their tax exposure.

The Overall Business Assessment: Spend ninety minutes with a client reviewing the results to an assessment that reveals the weaknesses in their small business.

■

The key to these short, one-off introductory sessions is that they solve a clear and pressing problem for your client. Because these are one-off sessions, the value you offer is significant, and the price is affordable. Your clients will be more likely to engage you for further coaching, including signing up for your flagship small group. Not only this, but the session itself will help build trust in you as a coach and increase the likelihood your client will sign up for your small group.

Make sure to list each of your entry-level products on your landing page. Listing the various entry-level sessions you offer demonstrates your comprehensive knowledge of how to grow a small business. If I were looking at your website and reading about all the problems you could help me solve, I'd have immediate trust that you know what you're talking about when it comes to growing a business.

Each of the entry-level products should be built as a plug-and-play session you can deliver that might include a worksheet they fill out as the session goes along. Turning your ninety-minute coaching call into a process that includes a deliverable is going to allow you to deliver the session over and over without having to prepare.

If you aren't a business coach, you can easily create a list of introductory-level products you can offer to make it easier for clients to enter into a coaching relationship with you. If you pull out a piece of paper right now, I bet you could come up with three entry-level products and, by tomorrow, be prepared to actually deliver those products. Don't overthink it. Start creating those entry-level products today.

USE AN ASSESSMENT TO BOTH QUALIFY YOUR CLIENTS AND CLOSE THE SALE OF THE SMALL GROUP PRODUCT

One of the more effective lead-generating products you can offer is a session in which your clients take a twenty-minute online assessment and then meet with you to review the results. Your assessment should surface all the problems the client will need to address in order to grow their business. Each of the areas that need work are then covered in your flagship small group.

After taking an assessment, your client will have a "problem list" that details all the areas of their business (or areas of coaching you offer) in which they are weak.

The "problem list" itself is of significant value to the client because, without the list, the client usually has a hard time realizing what's keeping their business from growing. Think of the assessment like a diagnostic check a mechanic might perform on an automobile or a doctor might perform on your body. The check itself has value, but what's of even greater value is the list of frameworks and procedures that will need to be installed in the business to solve the problems—all of which, of course, correspond with the frameworks and playbooks that will be covered in your flagship small group.

For instance, an assessment might reveal that the business has a confusing marketing message, a lack of strategic vision, vague or nonexistent job descriptions for team members, and a strapped-together cash flow process. The coach then will explain to the business owner that they need to create a new mission statement and a set of guiding principles, clarify their marketing message, overhaul their marketing collateral, install a management and productivity system so the business runs more efficiently, and install a cash flow management procedure that gives the business owner better optics into their finances.

From there, you can offer to waive the first month's payment for your flagship small group and then sign them up to join the upcoming cohort. Or, if the client wants individual attention, you can take them through the same curriculum, offering a one-on-one coaching retainer for $1,000 or more per month.

> Use entry-level products, such as an assessment and coaching session, to fill your flagship small group.

If you are not looking to be a business coach, an assessment may still be of great value to your clients and serve as a terrific entry-level product. Whether you're helping people manage their time, raise kids, enjoy a better marriage, give better presentations, or even build their own personal platform, an assessment is a terrific addition to your entry-level menu of products.

ONCE YOU HAVE YOUR FLAGSHIP PRODUCT AND A SELECTION OF LEAD-GENERATING PRODUCTS, BUILD OUT YOUR PRODUCT MENU TO ADD EVEN MORE VALUE FOR CLIENTS

After your first small group is underway you can begin adding to your menu of products.

Here are some examples of advanced products small business coaches can offer:

One-on-One Coaching Retainer: Twelve-month one-on-one coaching to overhaul your client's entire business. In these one-on-one meetings you can offer to help your client optimize their leadership, marketing, sales, product optimization, management system, cash flow, and plenty more. The one-on-one coaching product can be delivered through bimonthly meetings and, if you like, can extend for years. (Suggested price: $12,000)

The Guiding Principles Workshop: This workshop helps business owners generate a new mission statement, key characteristics, critical actions, core values, and so on, which amount to an overhauled vision for the small business. This workshop will normally be delivered to the leadership team in a full day session. (Suggested price $5,000 to $10,000)

The Marketing Strategy Workshop: The marketing workshop should help customers clarify their marketing message and then apply their new message to an entire marketing funnel, including a landing page, lead generators, and emails. (Suggested price: $5,000 to $10,000)

The Sales Optimization Workshop: You can deliver a sales training workshop that helps your clients' sales teams optimize their pipeline, communicate more clearly with clients, identify missed opportunities, and close more sales. (Suggested price: $5,000 to $10,000)

The Two-Day Small Business Growth Plan Workshop: This workshop would be open to any small business owner who wants to grow their business. Because the workshop can be offered to the public and the cost would be affordable, the workshop itself also works as a paid lead generator. In the workshop you will take participants through your overall growth plan (as an introduction to your frameworks and processes). Essentially, this workshop would slowly deliver your frameworks along with a checklist each business owner could use to transform their business. And, of course, when you're done delivering the workshop you'd be looking at a room full of candidates for your flagship small group. (Suggested price: $299)

■

Your product menu can offer many more products than these, including fractional CMO, CFO, or CMO roles or even consulting that will help your client sell their small business. The point is this: Have a menu of products ready to sell to customers as they "graduate" from your flagship small group offering.

COACH'S STORY

In early 2020, I was a fairly successful coach. I made consistent money selling one-to-one coaching services to ambitious female entrepreneurs who wanted to grow a business to consistent $10,000 months. Through this work I discovered that a business needs a Hell Yes! Offer (one that draws people in and sells itself before you ever even have a conversation about it), or offer suite, and having one helped business owners make significantly more money and operate their business more smoothly than those that did not.

In March 2020, the pandemic hit, and everyone started to build businesses online. In that moment I realized that my general business coaching with one offer was not going to cut it. I needed to go from a general business coach selling one product to a general audience, to a coach who solved a specific problem, for a specific person, with a suite of products that helped meet them where they were. The answer was creating a menu of products centered around the Hell Yes! Offer and the Hell Yes! Offer model that I created.

In a matter of weeks I created a menu of products that focused on showing people how to create and optimize their offers—starting with my free podcast, *It's Your Offer*; my six-month mastermind; one-to-one consulting; and all-inclusive luxury retreats. Almost immediately my ideal clients started coming rapidly, my programs started selling out, and the results we were helping people create—even in the height of the pandemic—were astounding. My clients were building businesses, creating magnetic offers, and increasing their revenue with ease and a diversified menu of products. My business took on a whole new trajectory when my income doubled in 2021 and 2022 and has continued to grow. I'm now an in-demand consultant who helps businesses identify the gaps in their business that can turn into golden opportunities by optimizing their offers for Hell Yes!

Having a cohesive, well-planned list of products centered around my Hell Yes! Offer has been one of the single most powerful tools in my business and in the businesses of my clients. When your offers are optimized for your ideal client and the problem you're solving, and are created around your unique solution, clients are able to easily come into your business, find out how you can help them, and buy the solution they've been looking for. The result—a business that flies fast and far through smooth air and a well-defined course—will lead you to predictable and consistent income that makes growth the most fun adventure of all.

—JESSICA MILLER,
business coach since 2016

CAN A COACH REALISTICALLY BUILD A $150,000 COACHING BUSINESS IN UNDER TWENTY-FOUR MONTHS?

How quickly can a new coach scale their coaching business past $150,000 per year? If they are willing to put in the work, and if they know exactly what to work on, this can be accomplished in under twenty-four months. In fact, many new coaches I've worked with have managed to hit a $150,000 run rate in under six months. How do they do it? Let's crunch the numbers.

The Path to $150,000 in Your First Six Months

Paid lead-generating assessment sessions or other introductory products: 2 sessions per month at $500 = $12,000.

1 flagship six-month small group: 20 total members at $5,000 per attendee = $100,000.

3 one-on-one coaching clients at $1,000 per month
= $36,000.

4 one-off workshops on various topics, such as guiding
principles, messaging, sales, and so on at $5,000 each
= $20,000.

TOTAL: $168,000

I hope you can see clearly how building a coaching business is
not only possible, it's realistic. And how many hours of your time
would it take to deliver the kind of value it takes to surpass
$150,000? Not as many as you might think. Let's break down the
exact same product offering as listed above with a focus on how
long it will take you to deliver those products.

Delivering the paid lead generators at 90 minutes each: 36
hours per year.

Delivering your flagship small group to 20 clients for 60
minutes, 6 times a year: 6 total hours per year.

Delivering one-on-one coaching for 3 clients at 60 minutes,
twice each month: 72 hours per year.

Delivering 4 all-day workshops at 8 hours per workshop:
32 hours per year.

When you add all the hours you will spend delivering this
value, it totals 146 hours. Now remember, this number is per
year so that is pretty low when you consider how many working
hours are in a year. In fact, if you work forty hours per week,

that means you're spending less than four weeks of eight-hour days delivering your coaching products and you still have eleven months of time to enjoy friends, family, hobbies, or to grow your coaching business even larger. Another way to look at how these hours could be delivered is that you'd only have to coach on Monday and Tuesday and you could take the rest of the week off.

Of course, as you're building your business, you will need to spend the other three days of your week adding clients to your potential client list, engaging in introductory coaching conversations, writing and sending emails, creating your menu of products, and actually preparing to deliver your coaching sessions.

That said, once your website is up and running, your lead generators have been created, your automated emails are written and working, your products exist, and you no longer need to prepare because you are always ready to coach at a moment's notice, you really will have what amounts to a part-time job that pays extremely well. The point is this: If you build a successful coaching business, you really could create your dream job.

HOW CAN YOU BUILD A MILLION-DOLLAR COACHING BUSINESS?

If you want to scale your coaching business even further, you can do so by simply hiring coaches to work under you and use the exact same playbook to grow their coaching hours that you used to fill yours.

For example, if you have four coaches who are each facilitating four ten-person flagship small groups and you charge $5,000 for each person, your gross revenue is $200,000 per coach, totaling $800,000 overall. If you pay each coach about $125,000, depending on how many small groups they lead, your profit will be $300,000. Add this to your workshops and your own elite small group and you will easily gross over $500,000.

Essentially what you are going to build if you hire coaches to work under you is a small coaching agency.

The way a coaching agency might look is this:

1. Use popular lead-generating collateral to build your list.

2. Sell paid introductory sessions to on-ramp customers and build trust.

3. Host one large conference (two hundred or more business owners) each year as a low-cost entry into your coaching services.

4. Upsell six-month small group memberships to your entire list, especially those who attend your conference. Have your coaches coach these small groups.

5. Upsell all small group members to your leadership, management, marketing, and sales workshops.

6. Further upsell clients to your personal, elite mastermind.

The staff required to pull off a model like this would simply be yourself, an executive assistant who could act as an event planner, a freelance marketing person, and four freelance coaches. And that's it. To be sure, that's a lot to manage, but if you like building a business and don't mind managing people, you could easily build a small coaching agency.

If you want to take your coaching agency even further—that is, into a seven- or eight-figure coaching business—I've included a playbook to do so at the end of this book. Growing an eight-figure coaching business will require hiring and managing a staff, and so the playbook you will find in the chapter on How to Scale Your Coaching Business to Seven Figures and Beyond was created in the form of a hiring plan, complete with job descriptions for each of your necessary hires.

At this point, you may be thinking that all of this seems overwhelming. All you want to do is grow a small coaching business with a small client list and a life you enjoy. Terrific. The truth is, you can easily accomplish that in a short period of time and then, if you choose, continue to grow into a small agency.

CREATING A MENU OF PRODUCTS WILL GIVE YOU THE CONFIDENCE YOU NEED TO BUILD A STRONG, STABLE COACHING BUSINESS

Here are six reasons creating a menu of products is the very first step to building a successful coaching business:

1. You will know what problems you can help a client solve because you've created products to solve them.

2. You will be able to ask for money with a great deal more confidence because you have something tangible to offer in exchange.

3. You will be able to deliver value at a moment's notice because you are already prepared with value to offer.

4. You will be able to plan the growth of your business, built on real sales goals and broken down by products.

5. You will increase referrals because your clients will know which of your services to recommend to their friends.

6. Your confidence as a small business coach will skyrocket because you will constantly be delivering incredible value to your clients.

CAN YOU REALLY ASK FOR THIS KIND OF MONEY IN EXCHANGE FOR COACHING?

Some coaches enjoy giving advice and counsel but feel uncomfortable asking for the money. When you create a menu of products, it's easier to ask for what you are worth because you're exchanging the money for tangible value in the form of a product. Successful coaches ask for the money with confidence. If you can help somebody make money, you are definitely worth money yourself. Let's practice what we preach. If there's one thing a business coach needs to do, it's help a client offer value in exchange for dollars and then teach them to collect and manage those dollars. Exchanging value for dollars is, after all, what every successful business is about. Your coaching business is no different.

Your clients are going to get an enormous return from their investment in your coaching. Just clarifying their marketing message alone could make them hundreds of thousands, if not millions. Learning to craft a sales pitch could make them millions more. Installing a cash flow playbook could save them from bankruptcy, and learning to manage their people might actually get them the psychological break they need to get some sleep and stay sane.

If you aren't a business coach, imagine how much joy you're bringing people by introducing them to a new hobby, or how much frustration you are saving by helping them introduce their newborn to an eating and sleeping schedule. Whether you're a photography coach or a math tutor, your coaching offers tangible value in that it improves the quality of your clients' lives.

The fact that you are delivering value isn't the only reason you should charge for your coaching services, however. Another reason to charge for your coaching services is because, if you don't charge, people will not respect you and they will not tell their friends about you.

As a general rule, people do not respect things they do not pay for.

You should charge for your coaching. And if you are able to deliver incredible results, you should charge a premium.

Coaching creates a win/win scenario for both the coach and clients—but especially for the clients. Not only this, the client benefit extends well beyond the time their coaching engagement ends.

For your clients, an investment in a good coach could pay lucrative dividends for decades to come.

SHOULD YOU DISCLOSE THE PRICE
OF YOUR PRODUCTS UP FRONT?

You do not need to share your prices up front but I strongly recommend doing so, especially if you are nervous about asking for a premium. If you are nervous about asking for a premium, you are likely going to reduce your prices in order to build your business. The problem with reducing your prices to build your business is that when you reduce your prices, you reduce the perceived value of your coaching. Also, when you disclose your prices right there on your website, you weed out clients who can't afford your services or simply want to enjoy your wisdom for free.

Your prices, of course, may vary based on many factors, including the amount of time your client will require, whether or not your client will need to meet in person, whether or not they will be in a small group or want to meet one-on-one, and, of course, the complexity of their problems.

If you would like to disclose prices but also want price flexibility, you can include verbiage such as "starting at $5k" to cover the necessary price customizations.

> When clients know how much they are required to pay for a specific product, they are much more likely to perceive the value of that product. Never devalue yourself or your products because when you do so, you devalue the perceived value your client is being offered.

HOW MUCH SHOULD YOU CHARGE
FOR YOUR SERVICES?

How much can you charge for your products and services? It's a great question. And of course the answer changes based on the needs of the person asking the question.

The amount of money you can charge for your products and services depends on one thing: how big of a return your client will receive after you've coached them. Whether it's a financial return or a quality of life return, you can charge more depending on the return you are able to deliver.

A good coach will get their client an enormous return on their investment. This is yet another reason to coach your clients using proven, dependable coaching products. Knowing what products you sell allows you to better understand what kinds of returns those products deliver.

As a business coach, I like to follow the 10 percent rule, meaning the price I charge for my coaching will be under 10 percent of the return I conservatively expect my client to get if they execute the playbook or framework I will help them install. In fact, I believe so passionately in the 10 percent rule that I offer a full refund on my coaching services if my client does not get a ten-times return on their investment from my coaching. That is an easy guarantee to make, however, because I won't work with a client who is not qualified to get a massive financial return. What I mean by that is I only take clients who have a good business, a good leadership team, the resources to push the plan we come up with, and the ability to actually make more money. If a client meets these criteria, I know I can come in and coach them to significant success and a significant return on their investment.

And besides, I'd gladly give a client their money back if they didn't get a return for no other reason than to protect my reputation as a coach. I do not want anybody walking around feeling they got a bad deal out of my coaching. As a coach, I am not looking for a winning record; I am looking for a perfect record.

Your coaching is a financial investment that should promise a financial return. If your client can earn a $100,000 return after you teach them how to create a terrific sales pitch, for example, you can safely charge $5,000 to $10,000 for that training. If your one-year mastermind is going to help clients achieve a 30 percent increase in revenue for their $1 to $3 million small businesses, you can charge each client $6,000 to attend the mastermind or even $1,000 each per month for one-on-one coaching.

Don't misunderstand me. You are not looking to charge 10 percent of whatever your clients make. No business is going to give you 10 percent of their sales. That said, if you are well under the 10 percent investment rule, I believe your products are fairly priced.

Some coaches, especially coaches who are just starting out, don't feel comfortable charging so much for their products and services. I understand. These prices can seem exorbitant, especially when you are talking about a workshop you can deliver in a single day. However, it bears repeating that those who are tempted to lower their prices in order to get more business should remember a basic principle that is true in all consumer markets: Human beings associate value with price.

Years ago, for example, I made most of my living traveling and speaking. It was a great life and I made a great living. However, when I got married and my wife and I started thinking about having a family, I knew I needed to come off the road. Instead of removing my speaking page, however, I asked my team to keep it up and simply double my speaking honorarium. Why? Because I knew nobody would hire me at such a high price and yet, by asking for the new price, I would increase the perceived value of my speaking. For me, raising my speaking honorarium was a value-perception strategy. And besides, if my invitations to speak were cut in half, I could make the same amount of money I made before, all while staying happily married.

You can guess what happened next. Just a few weeks into announcing my new speaking honorarium, speaking requests *increased*. That's right, the number of businesses and conferences that wanted me to come in actually went up. Why? Because people assumed I was worth it and they were looking for a very good speaker. When I went to tell my wife what had happened, she started packing my bag for me.

"With that kind of money, we can buy a great marriage!"

I'm kidding, of course. My wife and I did have to limit the number of speaking engagements I would accept in order to protect our life and our family, but the point is this: Charging more for my speaking helped my clients understand the value that I offered.

As you grow in competence and as you generate better and better results for your clients, you will be able to raise your price based on the proven value you are offering.

> Again, the bottom line is this: If you want to grow your
> coaching business, see yourself as a financial investment
> that generates significant returns for your clients.

As a small business coach, you sell money. You literally sell an increase in revenue, which amounts to money. If there was a store down the street where people could buy $1,000 for an investment of $500, do you think that business would do well? Of course it would. There would be a line around the block and down the street, every single day.

The key to growing your coaching business, then, is to make sure your coaching products get your clients a terrific return on their investment.

As you move further and further into your coaching business, your menu of products will evolve. You will naturally adjust your offerings and your prices based on customer demand and client feedback. This is normal. The point is to always know what it is you are offering, what problems your products solve, and what kind of return your clients can expect.

Once you create your list of products, you will start to feel much more confident about how you're going to succeed as a coach.

■

After you have a menu of products, it's time to start thinking about a potential client list. When starting out, most coaches think first about their potential client list, but I think this is a mistake. Your first step should be all about creating products because it's only after you create those products that you can fully recognize the clients who might need those exact products. In short, once you have created a menu of products, a list of potential clients will naturally fall into place.

In the next chapter, I'll guide you through the process of creating a potential client list and also show you how to organize and communicate to that list so you convert potential clients into paying customers.

STEP TWO

Create and Manage a Potential Client List

Now that you've created a list of coaching products you can offer, you'll want to create a list of qualified buyers who would benefit from those products. Essentially, you will want to keep an eye out for people you meet who are struggling with the very problems you and your products resolve.

As it relates to leading a business, nearly every business owner is struggling with something. After all, very few people start a business because they want to run a business. People start businesses because they want to be financially free, or because they're passionate about a product, or because they want to help people. If the business succeeds, however, they find themselves in foreign territory: They never actually learned how to operate a business.

How long will it take you to build a database of potential coaching clients? Not long. In fact, if you pulled out a sheet of paper and wrote down the names of every person you know or have met who runs a business, I bet you could get to ten or twenty names immediately, and many more the next day. Then, after your eyes are opened to the many people in your circle of influence who are attempting to run or grow a business, that list will triple or quadruple within a few weeks.

After you create a menu of products, qualified client leads will become more obvious. When Nicole Burke first started offering gardening advice, she showed up at her first client's house with a basket full of lettuce from her garden. The client happened to have four friends over and those friends became her very next clients.

> As word spreads about your expertise, your client list
> should begin to grow.

As a business coach, if you start a flagship small group, you will only need about twenty paying clients to get to a six-figure income and about twenty more to double that. That said, not everybody on your client list is going to engage you as a coach. Still, if only 10 percent of the people on your list make a purchase, that means you only need to collect two hundred names and email addresses in order to build a successful coaching business. That may seem like a lot, but honestly, don't you think you could build a list like that within a year?

There is enormous potential for you in the small business segment alone.

What sort of small business owners are you looking for? Real estate agents. Financial advisors. Dentists. Contractors. Lawn care providers. Potters. Artists. Insurance agents. Mortgage brokers. Gym owners. General practitioners. Restaurant owners. Artists' reps. Retail store owners. Bed-and-breakfast owners. Cleaners. Florists. Handymen. Mechanics. Plumbers. Window cleaners. Woodworkers. Consultants. Tailors. Freelance developers. Personal trainers. Dog trainers. Graphic designers. Videographers. Photographers. Counselors. Clothing boutique owners. Brewers. Specialty food store owners. Digital content creators. Social media influencers. Conference speakers. Nutritionists. Food truck owners. Car detailers. Arborists. Nursing home owners. Junk removers. Bankers. Lawyers. Writers. Travel agents. Home inspectors. Personal chefs. Property managers. Family doctors. Massage therapists. Interior designers. Nonprofit owners. Tour guides. Tutors. Event planners. Caterers. Coffee shop owners. Moving companies. Professional organizers. Daycare owners. The list is nearly endless. And these are only the small, small business owners. Truthfully, any business that is making less than $100 million will benefit from you as a small business coach, and that means there are more than thirty million potential clients in America alone.

Add to this list all the executives and managers at large businesses who may be looking to move up in their career. Those folks need coaches, too.

Once your eyes are open to entrepreneurs and business leaders who carry the burden of providing for themselves and their employees, you will see them everywhere. And you will write down their names and email addresses and begin to introduce them to the value you are able to offer in the form of nurture and sales email campaigns.

HOW DO YOU LAUNCH A COACHING BUSINESS?
YOU TELL PEOPLE YOU ARE A COACH.
OVER AND OVER.

It's important that you tell people you're a coach, especially if you are pivoting in your career. At first, the people who knew you in your previous work may have to grow accustomed to your new career, but after they hear you introduce yourself as a business coach or receive a few emails from you in which you offer business advice, their image of you will change. And the sooner people think of you as a business coach, the sooner people will engage in your services and tell their friends about your coaching.

In my experience, any change in career direction takes about three years to metabolize one's identity. I started out as a memoirist and moved into business writing and then into coaching coaches. Each transition has been easier than the last but it does take a little time. In truth, though, these transitions make sense. The world is fluid and so are you. As you grow in your professional career, you will always be building on the past to create a new and better future for yourself.

Not long ago, I spoke with a gentleman who was pivoting his career from an accountant to a business coach. He asked whether he should mention that he used to be an accountant or whether such an unrelated job damaged the authority that he needed to position himself as a coach.

"When you were an accountant, did you ever look at profit and loss statements that made you shake your head because of the obvious business mistakes the client was making?" I asked.

"All the time," he said.

"Great. Then all you need to say is that you used to be an accountant and got tired of reading profit and loss statements that revealed terrible business decisions so you moved into coaching to help people before they made all those terrible mistakes."

What this gentleman thought was a liability—that he was an accountant and had no coaching experience—was actually a massive asset. In his coaching, he'd be in a position to help people long before their profit and loss statements started looking so ugly.

> Your experience is a massive asset to help you build a career as a coach. Leverage that experience for the benefit of your clients.

If my new friend wants to grow his coaching business, all he needs to do is tell the story of how he got tired of seeing people make mistakes over and over until everybody he meets understands his backstory and how much he can help them generate more revenue and much better profit and loss statements.

After our accountant/coach friend tells his story, he can ask for a potential client's contact information and, later, email them and repeat the story, further "branding" himself as a business coach with the added experience of an accountant in the minds of everybody he meets.

In fact, this is how my personal business coach secured my business. And yes, I meet with a business coach twice each month. I pay thousands each year to meet with my coach, and the investment is worth every penny and more. The truth is, though, I never thought of my coach as a business coach before I hired him. He was an old friend I followed on Instagram. I loved the wisdom he shared on his Instagram feed and I'd read some of his books, but for whatever reason, I never thought of him as a coach. In fact, when I decided to hire a coach, I found myself thinking I could really use a coach like him. Then, one day, he reminded his followers that he was a business coach. It literally required him to say it that clearly before I even thought about contacting and hiring him.

If you are pivoting in your career, you may not think of yourself as a business coach. You just don't have the experience. But if you have the expertise, and you have the menu of products, you are a coach. It may take some time for your identity to catch up, but the fact is, you are now a coach.

HOW DO YOU BRAND YOURSELF
AS A BUSINESS COACH?

Another reason to start an email list is because it gives you the opportunity to further brand yourself by sending out emails that offer free value. Obviously, not everybody will hire you when they find out you are a business coach, but if they hear from you on a thoughtful, consistent basis, you greatly increase interest and demand for your coaching services.

Why? Because familiarity often corresponds with trust. People tend to buy products and services from leaders they are familiar with, and familiarity takes time. By collecting a list of leads and sending emails to those leads, you are creating a sense of familiarity and trust, which, over time, will lead to orders.

If you use the process I'll describe in this chapter, you will build a database of potential clients and earn their trust by sharing your knowledge through a simple, automated email system.

Even if your contacts never hire you, you'll position yourself as a business coach in their minds and word of mouth will spread.

If you're just getting started in coaching, creating a list of potential clients and staying in communication with those contacts is critical to growing a coaching business. I don't know of a single business coach who has created and nurtured a list of potential clients and failed to grow their coaching business. Every single coach who starts and maintains an email list grows their coaching business, and most of them grow it quickly.

Starting a list of potential clients and communicating with them regularly is something you can do even before you quit your day job. In fact, I have a friend who spent years as the CEO of a $100 million company and yet kept his own private customer relationship management system, staying in touch with thousands of friends and business leaders week after week. When my friend stepped down as CEO and started his own coaching business, he was able to contact that list about the new coaching products he offered and brought in over a half million dollars his first year as a coach. Why? Certainly he had a lot to offer but, more importantly, he had qualified leads with whom to extend those offers. Not only did he have qualified leads, he'd been nurturing those leads for years and so he'd earned the kind of trust required for clients to pay him a premium for his coaching products.

SUBSCRIBE TO A BASIC CRM AND
START BUILDING YOUR LIST TODAY

To nurture your email list, you will want to create a CRM. CRM is short for customer relationship management, and while it sounds complicated, it really isn't. Basically, a CRM is a database allowing you to email clients. Most CRMs can grow into much more robust relationship management and data tracking tools, but at its core, it's a tool allowing you to get and stay in touch with people.

Here are several things you can do to start and nurture a database of potential clients and create a community around your coaching platform:

- Subscribe to a CRM software provider and start adding names and email addresses to your database.

- Make a list of the top twenty challenges your clients face (and you solve) and create emails that offer solutions to those challenges.

- In your emails, list your coaching products and drive traffic back to your landing page as a way of introducing potential clients to your coaching services.

- Qualify and close leads by making direct offers to engage your introductory products to your flagship offer.

- Give clients a chance to engage with you, in person, in a nonpaying, informal breakfast or lunch.

- Deliver keynotes and webinars to secure new leads.

If you take these steps, you will grow your coaching business. It really is that simple. Once your CRM is established, growing your coaching business is as easy as adding email addresses to the database and allowing the CRM to do the work.

Maintaining your own CRM is a serious advantage in any business career.

In fact, even if you never intend to become a business coach, managing a CRM that includes potential clients' email addresses and staying in contact with them is a terrific career move. Imagine how much faster a person's career would rise if they sent out a monthly piece of business advice based on what they'd learned recently.

Staying in touch with your list of business contacts will do two things to catapult your coaching business: First, it will create reciprocity. Because you're sharing monthly or weekly coaching wisdom, you'll be generating gratitude among your followers and you'll be more likely to secure business when a client who has benefited from your free coaching encounters a significant challenge.

Second, and perhaps even more important, the potential clients who receive your emails will actually remember that you are a coach. Most of the people we meet in business come in and out of our network in minutes, not months. Just think about the last conference you attended. How many hands did you shake? How many people were you introduced to? How many people did you have lunch with? Now, how many of those people keep in touch with you once each week via an automated email campaign? Likely, none. Imagine if you'd met somebody two years ago and they had been sending you helpful coaching tips every month since then. How much more likely would you be to call them if you were struggling with a problem they addressed in a recent email?

At its core, business is a relational ecosystem. The longer you stay in relationship with people, the larger your network within that ecosystem will be and the more people will remember you when your expertise is needed.

We tend to do business with people who are familiar to us.

Keeping a personal CRM and staying in touch with people is just smart business.

Later in this book, I will show you the kind of emails you can send to potential clients. I'll even give you template emails you can send that will definitely grow your coaching business. For now, though, let's walk through the steps you need to take to create a foundation for your customer relationship management system.

CREATE AN ACCOUNT INSIDE A CUSTOMER RELATIONSHIP MANAGEMENT SYSTEM

I know what you're thinking. You're thinking that signing up for a CRM is something the marketing department should do. That's absolutely true. But if you're starting or running a coaching business, *you* are officially the marketing department. And also product development and sales and operations and the coffee runner.

It can be intimidating to think about managing a CRM but don't be intimidated at all. If you dive in and play with a CRM for a couple hours, you will love it forevermore. By setting up an account with a CRM provider, you will be stepping into a world you will enjoy. Not only that, you will have firsthand knowledge of a system you can coach clients to use as well.

There are many CRMs out there but not all of them are designed to help you manage a small database. Some CRMs, however, have low-price, entry-level subscriptions that will allow you to manage a customer list of dozens to hundreds of potential clients. The problem with most CRMs as they relate to a coaching business is they are too robust. Avoid those CRMs as you create your database. A couple years ago, I flew out to visit Keap, a CRM company out of Phoenix that specializes in small business. I liked them a lot and so I worked with them to create a plug-and-play CRM for coaches. The system includes dozens of email templates you can edit to customize for your coaching effort. It's terrific and you can get started with it at CoachBuilder.com.

If you subscribe to a CRM and spend a short morning playing around with the system, growing your business will feel more like playing a video game than a branding and marketing exercise. And if you get hooked on managing a CRM, your coaching business should grow a lot more quickly than if you simply rely on word of mouth alone.

MAKE A LIST OF THE TOP TWENTY CHALLENGES YOUR CUSTOMERS FACE AND CREATE EMAILS THAT OFFER SOLUTIONS TO THOSE CHALLENGES

Remember, clients will only hire you to help them solve problems. Think of that as good news, though. If you are clear about the problems you solve, people will hire you.

In fact, you can even segment your mailing list based on the problems different clients have. A client who lets you know they're dealing with management issues can get ten emails with management tips and then a sales email offering your fractional COO service. Meanwhile, a client with an underperforming sales team will get emails offering sales advice followed by a sales email offering your sales training workshop.

Remember, the reason to put these clients into your CRM is because this will allow you to slowly develop familiarity and trust, which will ultimately lead to sales.

So what problems should you define in order to segment your list? That depends. It depends on what problems you are qualified and skilled at helping customers resolve. If you want to enjoy your life as a coach, then you will want to help clients resolve problems that you absolutely *love* resolving.

To find out what problems your potential clients are struggling with, set up an automated survey inside your CRM. You can do this by making the third or fourth email in your nurture campaign a questionnaire asking about client pain points. For instance, you can ask potential clients which is the biggest challenge they are dealing with now:

- We need to generate more revenue.

- We are paying too much in taxes.

- Our marketing strategy isn't working.

- We aren't aligned around a common mission.

- Nobody really knows what they are supposed to be doing.

- We are not closing sales.

- Our profit margins are shrinking.

- We are losing market share to the competition.

The same kind of list can be created even if you are not a business coach. Every coach exists to do one thing: help people solve their problems. No matter what kind of coaching you do, make a list of problems and then begin offering advice on how to solve those problems inside an automated email campaign.

If you ask enough potential clients to identify their most pressing challenge, you will soon identify the pain points that will grow your coaching business the fastest.

If you don't want to create a survey and include it in your nurture campaign, you can generate a list of pressing challenges just by listening to your potential clients talk about their businesses.

Here are the phrases you will be listening for from potential clients that reveal the problems they are struggling with:

- **Leadership:** We are basically making it up as we go. Everybody is wearing a bunch of different hats.

- **Messaging and Marketing:** We aren't sure how to talk about what we offer and we need serious help getting the word out about what we do.

- **Sales:** We don't know how to close the big deal. Or any deal for that matter. We are basically just taking orders and hope that orders come in.

- **Products:** People love our products but they only buy one and then we never hear from them again.

- **Operations:** I need help organizing my company so it's less frustrating and more productive.

- **Cash Flow:** We are always running out of cash. Bills just seem to come out of nowhere.

The list above happens to reflect the six areas that create the biggest headaches for small business owners. Because these are the six areas most small business owners struggle with, again, you will want to create coaching products that help resolve each problem. I'll talk more about creating coaching products in a later chapter.

IN YOUR EMAILS, LIST YOUR COACHING PRODUCTS AND DRIVE TRAFFIC BACK TO YOUR LANDING PAGE AS A WAY OF SECURING ORDERS FOR YOUR COACHING PRODUCTS

As you begin to create emails that nurture clients, you will be tempted to give away the answers for free. Don't. The general rule about email marketing is that you give away the "why" but sell the "how." What does this mean? It means you can talk endlessly about how important it is to clarify your marketing message and even show before and after examples of what a clear message looks like, but save the actual exercise the clients will go through to clarify their own message for a paid session. If a potential client wants to experience the same transformation you demonstrated in your nurture emails, they will need to contact you and sign up for your small group or perhaps even book a private workshop.

Revealing the *why* but selling the *how* may sound like you are withholding value from the client, but in truth you are not. Most of your potential clients will not have realized their message was unclear until they read your email. Letting a potential client know what's holding them back is valuable in itself. To get the solution, though, they will need to purchase your time and expertise.

The gist of a nurture campaign is this: It should help potential clients diagnose and "feel" their problems, which, in turn, will increase the perceived value of your products.

CLOSE LEADS BY MAKING AN OFFER

Many coaches make the mistake of helping clients realize they have a problem but failing to list the products those clients can buy that resolve those problems.

Even though the email campaign you are creating is a nurture campaign, designed to build familiarity and trust, you will want to talk about the relevant products you sell anyway. If you like, you can do this with the addition of a simple postscript. At the end of each nurture email, simply include a line like this: *P.S. I will be helping my coaching clients resolve their team alignment problem by coaching them through the creation of a new mission statement in our first small group meeting. If you've not signed up for my coaching small group yet, you can do so HERE.*

A line like this at the end of each email will allow potential clients to connect their problems to your products and also encourage them to buy those products. Remember, you are not in the business of giving free coaching advice. You are in the business of selling your coaching advice. If you want to sell more of your coaching services, talk about your products in your emails and then make it easy for people to buy them.

DEFINE YOUR COACHING SPECIALTY

As your client list grows and clients begin to pay for your coaching products, you will find you specialize in about three areas.

This is almost always the case. While a good small business coach can help a client resolve hundreds of problems, many coaches migrate toward only a few areas of expertise.

Over time, you will find you get clients their largest returns when you coach them through your strongest competencies, whether that's managing their cash flow or installing an operations and management playbook. Your areas of expertise will surface, if they haven't already. This will be helpful in building your coaching business because the more your clients see returns on their investment in you, the more confidence you will get as a coach and the more word will spread about your abilities.

Again, in your first year of coaching, I recommend defining three areas in which you deliver the best possible results and I recommend getting better and better at those three areas. Of course you may always be a generalist, but the three areas in which you get your clients the largest returns will become the wide doors through which clients walk as a way of engaging your coaching services.

BUILD YOUR COACHING BUSINESS BY ASKING THE RIGHT QUESTIONS

Potential clients may not realize they need a coach. Most small business owners are so busy trying not to drown they don't realize they never learned to swim.

Once you've chosen three problem areas to focus on, you will want to memorize three defined, repeatable questions you can ask to qualify potential clients and help them realize they have the problems you resolve.

For instance, if you've chosen to sell a fractional COO product in which you help businesses install an operations and management playbook, you might ask potential clients a question like this:

"Does every member of your team have a clear job description or do you feel like people are making it up as they go along?"

If your potential client expresses frustration about how hard it is to organize their team and keep everybody productive, you'll simply say:

"I have a process that will solve that problem. I have a management playbook you can install in about ninety days. Give me your card and I'll send you some information."

At that point you take the potential client's card, write "management" on the back, and when you're back at your computer, you'll send them an email saying it was great to meet, let them know you're going to send them some emails that will help them with their management and productivity system, and enter them into that segmented list in your database.

That potential client will then be sent five or six emails in which you will provide a helpful understanding of what a small business management playbook could look like. And, of course, remind them you can come on for six months as a fractional COO, a product you sell for a fixed fee.

You will find that when you help a client identify their problem, position your product as the solution to that problem, and then earn trust and familiarity with a specific nurture campaign, clients place orders.

Once you have your qualifying questions down and your nurture email campaigns in place, building your coaching business is as simple as engaging in conversations and following up with qualified leads.

If you ask the qualifying question to ten potential clients, one of them, after receiving a few of your emails, is going to call you and say, "Hey, I got your latest email and I'd love to know more about this fractional COO consulting. We're a mess over here." At that point, you'll explain how it works and close the deal.

Here are some qualifying questions to ask based on the six most pressing problems your business clients likely struggle with:

Leadership: *Is your business focused on three economic priorities or does it feel like you are always diving for dollars?*

Marketing and Messaging: *Is your marketing working or are you struggling to get the word out about what you offer?*

Sales: *Do you think your sales effort could be more effective or is your team closing big sales every day?*

Product Optimization: *Does it seem like your profit margins have been shrinking?*

Management and Operations: *Do you have a repeatable set of meetings that allow you to organize and inform your team so you can reach your goals?*

Cash Flow: *Do you feel good about your rainy-day fund or do you always feel like you're treading water financially?*

HOW TO ANNOUNCE THAT YOU ARE
PIVOTING TO A COACHING CAREER

Your search for qualified leads is more than an effort to grow your business; it's an effort to build a community of small business owners you can shepherd to success. In fact, if you see your job as that of a community builder, your coaching business will build itself.

Think of your CRM as a community-building tool.

Here are some ideas that will help use your CRM to build a community:

As you launch your coaching business, send an email to everybody in your CRM explaining what you do and ask them to refer you to a friend. A good formula for this email might look something like this:

1. A greeting and an announcement that you are starting (or growing) a coaching business.

2. A list of the main problems you help people resolve.

3. A testimony of success in helping a client solve one or multiple of those problems.

4. A call to action.

5. A request for referral.

Here's an example of what this email could look like:

■ **DEAR FRIEND,**

As you may know, I've been happily employed at Acme Publishing for decades. My time at Acme was terrific and I'm grateful for the many relationships I built there.

Last year I decided to leave Acme in order to leverage my expertise and help more people with their publishing and book promotion needs. This is the part of my work at Acme I enjoyed the most.

Specifically, as a coach, I can help you or anybody you know through these challenges:

- Writing the book.
- Titling the book.
- Preparing the book for a publisher or for self-publishing.
- Negotiating a contract with a publisher that benefits you the most.
- Launching the book so it sells the most possible copies during release week.
- Getting covered by the media.
- Doing a terrific media interview.
- Leveraging your book into a speaking and consulting career.

Here's what bestselling author Amy Marks said about our coaching sessions:

"Without his help, I'd never have written the book, much less made it to the bestsellers list. His system is awesome, easy to follow, and effective. I'm grateful for his help."

If you are thinking of writing a book, click HERE so I can better understand what you're dreaming about. And if you know a friend who has talked recently about writing a book, do me (and them) a favor and forward them this email. I'd love to hear more about their dream of writing a book, too.

Here's to bringing better books into the world. Perhaps the next one will be yours!

Sincerely,

DONALD MILLER

Here's another example of what an email could look like if you already have a coaching business but would like to expand your coaching offers into other fields of expertise:

■ **DEAR FRIEND,**

As you may know, I've decided to coach people to help them write a book, which has been a terrific experience. That said, I've noticed as I've helped people write books, they also need help managing their teams. If you're trying to build a personal platform, managing a small team is paramount to your success.

If you or a friend are struggling with managing your team, I'd love to help.

Learning to manage your people will solve 80 percent of the problems that keep small business owners up at night. Through my mastermind, I've been able to help five small business owners align their team around a common mission, install five meetings that replace the hundreds of meetings that steal their freedom, and, most importantly, convert every employee into a profit-producing member of the team.

I'm adding another mastermind to my schedule this fall, which means I have room for five more small business owners.

If you're interested in talking about how I can help you grow your business, feel free to give me a call. If you have a friend who has recently mentioned they could use some help, especially with managing their team, forward this email to them and ask them to reach out.

It's difficult to grow a small business, but it's a lot easier when you resolve your management issues.

You can reach me at XXX-XXX-XXXX. Or, simply hit *reply* and I'll reach out to you.

Here's to the growing of your business by managing your team with confidence,

DONALD MILLER

An email describing a problem and offering a product as a solution will prove effective for you. My friend Brad, a very talented and experienced friend who left his position as a sales director, sent an email like this, and within six months was billing $45,000 per month in coaching and consulting. You will be surprised at how well a simple email like the ones I created above will grow your coaching business.

After you collect a potential client's email address, and after that client starts opening and reading your email, they still may not make a purchase from you. Because of this, you will want to invite them into a safe, risk-free taste of your coaching in the form of a small community you will curate and foster.

To be sure, giving you their email address and reading those emails are a kind of commitment; it's just not a financial commitment yet. If your coaching is expensive, it isn't an impulse buy. You will need to establish more trust.

The next thing you can get nonpaying clients to commit to, then, is to show up and meet you, and perhaps some of your other clients, in person. While this is still not a financial commitment on their part, it's a commitment that should be taken seriously. If they are willing to show up and meet with you, they are very close to paying you to do so on a regular basis.

HOST AN INFORMAL MONTHLY BREAKFAST

Another idea that will help you build your coaching business is to host a monthly breakfast. Think of your monthly breakfast as more of a community-building tool than a business-building tool, knowing that your business will grow out of your community.

In fact, you can make this breakfast a regular, recurring event by, say, hosting it on the first Monday morning of every month.

The key here is to invite both clients and potential clients so those you are coaching can mix with those who are considering hiring you as a coach. This monthly breakfast is a wonderful service to potential clients because it allows them to dip their toes in the water without having to make a commitment.

Again, the monthly breakfast should be reserved for existing clients and serious candidates only. Why is it so important that potential clients experience a little bit of your community? Some of your coaching products are going to cost ten, twenty, and perhaps even thirty thousand dollars. These are not impulse buys. In order to place an order like that, clients are going to have to have received emails from you that offer serious value and will want to see firsthand the sort of community you've created.

To ask qualified clients to join your breakfast, simply say, *"I host a small group of business owners once a month for breakfast. We talk a lot about how to solve some of the problems you're struggling with. I'd love for you to join us. We meet at Stay Golden over on Sidco Lane on Monday morning at 7:00 a.m. Do you have time to join us?"*

Even if your potential client only comes to one breakfast, they will likely remember you years later when they begin to struggle with an issue they know you can help them with.

Feel free to mention your monthly breakfast in your nurture emails. You will be surprised at how many potential clients show up to your breakfast after hearing about it four or five times in your emails.

At the breakfast, and in general with potential clients, try not to talk about your own goals and the struggles you are experiencing as you grow your coaching business. You can talk about that stuff in the community you have with fellow coaches. This breakfast is all about the client and should essentially amount to a group coaching discussion so small business owners feel (and are) less alone. Consider the breakfast a free sample of what your coaching small group looks and feels like but do follow up with new guests to invite them into your paying community.

DELIVER KEYNOTE PRESENTATIONS

Yet another way to build your coaching community is to deliver keynote presentations.

If you've developed a good introductory keynote, you should deliver that presentation at conferences where business leaders congregate. You can create a keynote on any or all of the areas in which you offer coaching, and when you're done speaking, collect leads from the room.

Here are several tips about giving a great presentation and using that presentation to collect leads:

- **Start the presentation by talking about the problem you solve.** An attention-grabbing statement to open your keynote will engage an audience. For example: "Over 80 percent of small business owners will be surprised by a tax bill or a vendor bill this year. But surprise bills shouldn't worry you. Not if you use five checking accounts to manage your cash flow."

- **Feature a lead generator with a QR code in the middle and at the end of your presentation.** We've found you'll get a 100 percent increase in the number of people who give you their email address if you feature a lead generator and do so twice during your presentation. The first time you feature your lead generator, you're seeding the idea; and the second time you feature it, you're giving people a final chance to receive it. I've had up to 98 percent of an audience opt in for my lead generator when I featured the lead generator itself twice in my presentation.

- **Restate the problem you can help people solve as the final statement in your presentation,** then let them know what lead generator you're offering that will help them solve that problem. Your last words will ring for a long time in your audience's ears, so use them wisely. If your last words are, "You don't have to struggle with cash flow, even if you aren't a numbers person. Using these five checking accounts to manage your business will save you thousands of dollars and dozens of sleepless nights. Download my PDF today and I'll walk you through how to set it up," you are going to get a great deal more business.

DELIVER WEBINARS

Similar to delivering keynote presentations, you can also deliver webinars.

Even before you speak at events, you can deliver your own webinars. These days you can deliver a webinar using nothing more than your smartphone and a keynote deck. A webinar is really just a keynote delivered for free on the internet and so it's also a great place to practice your skills as a presenter.

OFFER AN ASSESSMENT

Another way to generate leads is to offer a free, thirty-minute business assessment. In the first six or seven minutes of the assessment, ask questions that will reveal whether the potential client is struggling with any of the problems you solve. If they are, explain the framework they need to install and let them know about the coaching products you offer that will help them solve their problems. Many of the coaches in the community I created all use the same assessment at MyBusinessReport.com—it has been incredibly helpful as a tool to grow our various coaching businesses.

Remember, as you collect leads you will likely only need about fifteen to twenty paying clients to create a coaching business that will allow you to build personal wealth. If you can convert 10 percent of potential clients into paying clients, that means you only need to collect one hundred leads. Using the tactics I've talked about in this chapter, you should be able to do that in a short period of time.

ASK FOR REFERRALS

If you have an existing client base, feel free to ask them to invite their friends to the monthly breakfast or to attend a webinar. If you've delivered great coaching value to a client, they will not mind telling their friends about you, especially if you give them the opportunity to invite their friends to something specific. For example, every March you could host a webinar about tax strategies that are specific to small business owners. All you need to do, then, is let your current client list know about the webinar and send them some cut-and-paste copy they can use to invite their friends.

The opportunities for you to grow your community are endless. And if you're just starting out, you want to pursue them all. If you think of your primary objective as building a community and your secondary objective as building your paying client base, you will succeed.

Your networking and list building may seem slow at first, but I promise at the end of every month you will be surprised at how many business cards, emails, and phone numbers you've collected and added to your CRM.

BECOME A LEAD-GENERATING MACHINE

Without lead generators, a CRM, a segmented list, and subsequent follow-up emails, you will struggle to grow your coaching business. Yes, it's possible to grow your coaching business through word of mouth, but it will not grow as fast as it will by using a CRM, and besides, using a CRM will give you a more widespread impact because you've automated the wisdom and value you offer as a coach.

Once your CRM is created, your lead qualifying should take very little of your time. In fact, the only time you will have to spend warming up a qualified lead is the time it takes to ask a question, listen to the answer, and enter that prospect's name and email address into the appropriate segment of your CRM.

> Once your CRM is created, qualifying a lead and nurturing that lead will take you about two minutes per lead.

After you have created your CRM, you will likely be wondering where to send those clients so they can choose from your menu of products. In the next two chapters, I am going to help you get your website right (so it helps you close sales) and then I'll show you some sample emails you can send to close the deal.

STEP THREE

Get Your Website
(Sales Pitch) Right

fter you have a conversation with a potential client, send them to a landing page that clearly introduces them to your coaching products.

The job of your website is to deliver a sales pitch that gives a potential client the opportunity to accept or reject the challenge of working with you. If they accept the challenge of working with you, great. They're going to make a lot of money because that's what you know how to help them do. If they don't accept the challenge of working with you, they will have read your offer and will remember it months or years later when they finally realize they need a coach.

So far, most of your communication with potential clients has been pieced out over casual conversations, an email nurture campaign, and word of mouth. The reason potential clients will visit your website, then, is to see what all of this coaching talk is about. For this reason, your coaching website needs to do three things:

1. Clearly communicate the value you offer.

2. Display your menu of products.

3. Explain the steps a potential client can take in order to engage you as a coach.

Sadly, most coaches don't have a website at all. I get it. How good can a coach be if they have to promote themselves, right? Won't a good coach grow their coaching business through word of mouth? If you think about it, though, not creating a website and hoping your coaching business will grow through word of mouth is really about two things: pride and fear. Our pride wants people to wait in line for our services without us even having to promote ourselves, and our fear doesn't want to make a firm offer on a website because, well, we don't exactly believe in ourselves enough to sell ourselves.

As you know, 65 percent of small businesses fail and at least that many coaching businesses fail. One of the reasons coaching businesses fail is because the coach gives in to pride or fear. The humble, confident thing to do when building any small business is to express your offer clearly and confidently in the form of a website.

THE BENEFITS OF HAVING A COACHING WEBSITE GO BEYOND BASIC BUSINESS BUILDING

Another reason to create a website is because a website is standard for almost any business that wants to succeed. Your coaching clients will need a clear and compelling website in order to grow their businesses and so you will likely need to coach them regarding what that website needs to do and say. If your coaching clients notice you do not have a website, they will wonder why you don't practice what you preach. If nothing else, by having a website you will provide an example to your clients of how to boldly sell their products and grow their own businesses.

The main reason I think you should create a website, however, is because by doing so you will build more confidence in your coaching abilities.

The process of wireframing a good coaching website, which I will take you through in this chapter, is going to help you internalize the extreme value you offer as a coach. You will know what you are supposed to be competent in to deliver and so will the world. You will also collect testimonials about the successes you've helped others achieve and you will place those testimonials on your website so that everybody knows who you are and what you can do. Instead of hiding your competencies and hoping word of mouth spreads, you will use your website to put words in people's mouths to ensure people are talking about you and they are saying and thinking what you want them to say and think.

YOUR WEBSITE IS AN IMPORTANT BABY STEP IN YOUR CLIENT'S BUYING JOURNEY

Your website will also act as another step people can take to enter into the coaching community you have created. Your website might also be the main way you collect leads. If a potential client visits your website and is not ready to place an order, for example, you will ask them to download a PDF that gives them free, valuable information. Then later, through an email campaign, you will sell them one of your coaching products.

For most business owners, deciding to hire a coach is not an impulse decision. Coaching is often expensive and, besides the money, it will require a significant time commitment. To make a decision like this, potential clients will need to understand exactly what they're getting and why what they're getting is worth the investment. There is no place you are going to be able to make your offer so clear other than your website. When a potential client comes to your website, they are *expecting* you to pitch them on your services. If you fail to do so, they will not respect you or your offer and they will turn to somebody else for help.

If you want to see samples of coaching websites that work, my team and I put together a PDF of our favorite twenty-seven coaching websites. Each of these sites was created by coaches who are making more than $100,000 in their coaching businesses. Many of them, in fact, are making four or five times that amount. If you'd like to see samples of coaching websites that work, grab the PDF at CoachBuilder.com.

While your website can contain many ideas and images, let's look at seven sections every business coach should include in order to interest potential clients and convert them to paying customers.

LET'S WIREFRAME YOUR WEBSITE

The first step when it comes to creating a great website is to wireframe your site so it accurately reflects your unique offer to the world. A wireframe is a text-only rough draft of your website. The text, after all, is the hardest (and most important) part to get right. Your designer can add the logos, fonts, images, and color selections once your wireframe has been created, but without a strong offer in the form of actual words, you will not grow your coaching business.

The words on your website are just as important as the color scheme, style, and design of the website itself. Customers do not only place orders based on the feel of your brand, they place orders based on the words they read that make them want to place orders.

YOUR WEBSITE SHOULD FLOW LIKE A GOOD SALES PITCH

Coaching relationships are just like any other relationship in that they move through three phases. The first phase is curiosity, the second is enlightenment, and the third is commitment.

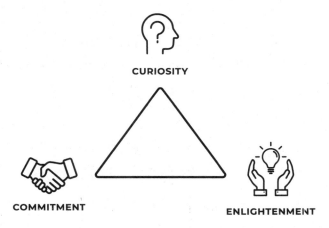

If we want to close sales, we have to guide potential clients through the three phases of every healthy relationship. We will do that on our website, in our lead generators, and through our nurture email campaigns.

As it relates to coaching, potential clients will only be curious about you if they realize you can help them survive and thrive. Specifically, if you are a business coach, they must realize all the ways you can help them grow their small business. After you pique your future clients' curiosity, they will want to know exactly how you can help them grow their business and will continue reading in hopes you will enlighten them. After they are enlightened, and only after they are enlightened, they will decide to commit, which means they will hire you to be their coach.

You cannot skip a phase in the relationship. If you jump to a request for a commitment too soon, your potential client will walk away as fast as somebody would walk away if you asked them to marry you on the first date. These things take time, and rightly so. Coaching is a serious commitment and investment.

As your potential client scrolls down your website, each section should feel like a sequential encounter. What I mean is, the first section of your website is like a first date, meaning you are really only letting the client know, in broad strokes, how you can help them. The second section is like a second date and so you can say a bit more about what you offer. The third section will allow you to say even more, and so on and so on. The longer a potential client stays on your website, the more they are interested in your services and so the more text you can use to explain what you offer.

The website I am about to walk you through, along with the lead generator and the subsequent follow-up emails you will create in a later chapter, are designed to pique your customers' curiosity, enlighten them about how you can help them grow their business, and invite them to commit by engaging in a coaching relationship with you.

The overall goal of your website is to invite customers into a story in which their problems can be solved and their lives can be enhanced by engaging you as their coach. If you keep that central idea in mind, your website will produce clients.

■

The copy on this example website uses marketing language and copy designed for a business coach. For the best success, edit the copy for your own coaching service.

You can certainly get creative when it comes to making a website, but here is the structure and order I recommend:

SECTION ONE: THE HEADER

The header is the top section of your website. It's the first thing people see when they visit your domain. In order to engage your future clients' curiosity, your header should clearly communicate three things:

1. **What you offer:** The first thing you've got to do in the header of your website is tell people exactly what business you are in. You're a coach. Specifically, you're a small business coach. Don't assume people know what you do just because you told them forty-seven times. When you're making casual conversation, most people aren't listening and so you will need to repeat what you offer multiple times if you are sure to be understood. In the header on your website, then, let

them know you are a coach and they can get coached by you in one-on-one sessions, masterminds, small groups, or in workshops (that is if you want to facilitate workshops).

2. **How what you offer can make your future clients' lives better:** Nobody wants to sign up for coaching, but everybody wants to sign up to see their business grow. Don't assume people know the results they will encounter if they engage your services. Instead, tell them. If you are a small business coach, you will help them increase revenue and profit. And more than this, you will deliver peace of mind, a good night's sleep, high team morale, work-life balance, and a business they can be proud of. Don't trust that future clients will figure out what you offer for themselves. If you don't tell your clients how you will change their lives, they will never understand why they should buy anything from you at all.

3. **What they need to do to work with you:** Let potential clients know what the next step will be if they want to do business with you. Do they need to call you, fill out an application, or engage in a thirty-minute intake call? Many coaches have lost a client, even though the client wanted to engage in a coaching relationship, just because the coach didn't give them clear instructions about how to engage their coaching services.

Don't worry about doing much more than communicating these three ideas in the header of your website. Remember, the header is the first date. Your job in the header of your website is to do one thing: pique your future clients' curiosity about how you can help them grow their business.

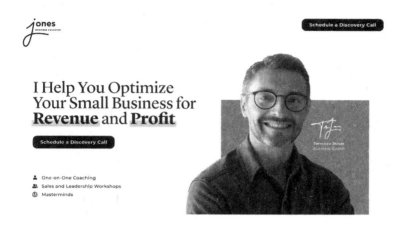

Notes on the Header Section

While using very few words, this header lets the future client know what the coach offers, how it can make their life better, and what the future client needs to do to engage the coach's services. That is, the coach offers small business coaching, does this through one-on-one coaching, workshops, and masterminds, and if the client engages the coach, the coach will help them optimize their business for revenue and profit. Also, the call to action is clear: Schedule a discovery call. When the header of a website is this simple and straightforward, there is no confusion about what this coach does, what products the coach sells, and how the client will benefit. A header like this should pique a client's curiosity, and when it does, they will scroll down the page to be further enlightened about why (and how) your coaching might work for them.

SECTION TWO: THE STAKES

Now that you've offered your potential client value, you'll want to remind them there are stakes at play if they don't take you up on your offer. The reason you want to include stakes in the story you are inviting future clients into is because, by including stakes, you communicate the urgency involved in engaging your coaching services.

By describing the problems and frustrations you help small business owners avoid, you are also letting them know what problems you can help the client solve and you are increasing the perceived value of your coaching products (the harder a problem is to solve, the more valuable the product that solves it will be).

The stakes section of your website could look something like this:

Notes on the Stakes Section

Your ability to solve the problems your potential clients struggle with is the only reason they will want to engage your coaching services. If you spell out those challenges clearly, clients will be more likely to hit your "call to action" button. Remember, the problem is the hook. As soon as a future client identifies their problem on your website, they start paying attention. If you do not talk about your potential clients' problems, they will bounce from your website and seek a solution to their problem elsewhere.

SECTION THREE: THE MENU OF SERVICES

Think about all the value you've communicated so far on this landing page. You've made a clear offer, told the potential client what problems you can help them solve, and you've invited them to take a small, easy step toward engaging you as a coach. Most coaching websites (that is, if the coach even has a site) aren't this clear, and yet you aren't even finished.

By the time your future client gets to the third section of your website, they're already on the third date. They're interested. They're willing to spend more time with you. This means you can talk a little bit more about what you offer and explain your services in more detail. You've earned the right to be heard.

Now that you've let them know what you offer and what problems you can help them solve, let's spell out the value in practical terms so they know exactly what their life is going to look like if they hire you as a coach. Let's give your future clients a list of products they can engage in order to solve their problems.

My clients can engage me to help them grow their
businesses in **five different ways**:

DIY Small Business Flight School

COST $2,500

In this six-month virtual experience, you
will get one video and exercise each week
along with a checklist of things you can do
to grow your small business. Click below to
start now.

Register Now

Small Business Flight School Mastermind

COST $5,000

The Small Business Flight School
Mastermind meets in person, once each
week, to discuss that week's exercise.
Flight School Masterminds cost $5,000. To
register, click below.

Register Now

One-on-One Flight School Coaching

COST $7,500

Meet with me one-on-one to optimize your
business for revenue and profit. If you'd
rather have my undivided attention than
work inside a small group, this option is for
you. You can apply for my one-on-one
coaching slots by clicking the button below.

Apply Now

Guiding Principles Workshop

COST $7,500

Everything starts with a compelling vision. If
you'd like to overhaul your guiding principles,
that is your mission statement, core values,
and more, we can get it done in a single day.
Sign up for a Guiding Principles Workshop
below.

Sign Up Now

Sales Training Workshop

COST $7,500

Most sales training is philosophical, but ours is practical. We are going to open up our computers and
email customers right there in the room. I will teach you to talk to customers in such a way they start
placing orders. Click below to book a workshop.

Book a Workshop

Notes on the Menu of Services Section

Be careful you don't say too much about your products here. Your potential client will be scanning your website so if you use too much text, they may tire of reading and move on. Simply print a brief description of your product. Or perhaps make each product a link so that it goes to its own landing page in which you pitch that specific product.

SECTION FOUR: PROOF OF VALUE

Now that your clients know what you offer and understand how you can change their lives, they will have one question: *Will coaching work for me?*

In order to demonstrate your coaching products will work for a potential client, consider including statistics and testimonials.

For instance, if 47 percent of your clients double their revenue after joining your flagship mastermind, place that information in this section of your website. If another 23 percent experience at least a 50 percent increase in overall revenue after attending your mastermind, make that information clear, too.

> Statistics offer proof of value. As you collect statistics about your clients' success, you will want to display that proof here.

If you don't have any statistics yet, consider including testimonials. Testimonials are equally as valuable as statistics. When a future client reads about one of your past clients who experienced success through your coaching, they see that client as a future version of themselves, especially if they are a similar-size small business or are in a similar industry. When you include testimonials, then, be sure to include a variety of businesses including *business to business* and *business to consumer* businesses. Also, if possible, make sure to include online businesses, brick-and-mortar retail stores, and even service industry businesses.

> The idea is this: You want your future clients to "see themselves" in the testimonials on your website.

Don't worry if you don't have many testimonials. You can literally start with one and add more as you change more lives.

Growing your small business with a coach means you grow your small business faster and stronger.

When we work together, we will clarify your mission, optimize your marketing, help you close more sales, refine your product offering, streamline your operations, and shore up your cash flow. If you want to sleep better at night, schedule an intake session today.

48%
... of small businesses double their revenue after having gone through my Small Business Flight School Mastermind.

71%
... of small businesses see a 50% or greater increase in revenue after attending Small Business Flight School.

98%
... of small businesses earn their coaching investment back, plus at least a 5X return on that investment within a year of engaging my coaching.

*"Ever since I hired Terrence to be my coach, my life has been more exciting and less stressful. My business is **growing** and I have a plan to **make it grow even more.**"*

Dave McCormick
owner of Acme Music Publishing

Schedule a Discovery Call

That said, don't forget to keep collecting testimonials. The more testimonials, the better.

Notes on the Proof of Value Section

Every good story has what's called a "climactic scene" and it's foreshadowed throughout the story itself. We know at the beginning of a movie, for instance, the climactic scene will have the hero defeating the villain and then disarming the bomb, or the couple in love will get married. By foreshadowing a climactic scene, the storyteller piques the audience's curiosity as to how, and whether, the scene will actually happen. In the proof of value portion of your website, you're essentially foreshadowing a climactic scene your potential client can imagine for their lives. By imagining a climactic scene in their lives, they are more likely to step into the story you're inviting them into because they have visualized and better understand where you can take them.

SECTION FIVE: THE PLAN

At this point, your pitch is going great. Your potential clients know exactly what you offer, exactly why it matters to them, and exactly what they need to do to take the next step. But many of your potential clients are still not going to make a purchase. Why? Because change is scary. And coaching is expensive.

What we want to do next, then, is build a bridge from the customer's problem (their business isn't growing at the pace they want it to grow) to your solution (the coaching products you offer can get their business growing again). To build that bridge, we are going to give our potential clients baby steps they can take to engage our services.

Very few people are going to read about your coaching services and then pull out their credit card to place an order. However, plenty of people may want to take a small step in that direction. After they take one step, they are more likely to take another, and once they've taken a couple steps, they're more likely to take the final step and commit.

When you include a three-step plan on your website, you break down the process of working with you into smaller investments of time and money that make the commitment of working with a coach less intimidating.

Working with a Coach is **Easy**!

Schedule an intake call

In a thirty-minute intake call, you and I will talk about what's holding you back and where you want your business to go.

Get a custom report

I'll send you a custom report about how we could work together to grow your small business. Growing a business is much easer if you have a plan. In step two, I will show you your plan.

Enjoy a growing business

In only six months you will not recognize yourself or your business. You will move from chaos to efficiency and from confusion to confidence. And you will make more money.

Schedule a Discovery Call

Notes on the Three-Step Plan Section

Giving potential clients baby steps increases the chances they will hire you. Be careful how many steps you give them, though. Including more than three steps might intimidate potential clients. The key to this section of the website is to make the process of hiring and working with you look simple, safe, and easy. In addition, including a three-step plan offers your future client a next step that is much easier to take than the giant commitment of hiring you right now.

> The three-step plan is a bridge. Very few people will figure out how to cross the ravine to hire you unless you build a bridge. Use a three-step plan to build that bridge.

SECTION SIX: THE EXPLANATORY PARAGRAPH

If you include the previous five sections on your website, many potential clients will hire you. Still, there are a few clients out there who will want to do due diligence before spending the kind of money it takes to hire a coach. For those who like to do a little research, what you need is a long-form, conversational explanation of why working with you as a coach is so important.

I've had many, many clients tell me they only decided to purchase my services after reading the explanatory paragraph section on one of my landing pages. Why? I think there are two reasons: The first is the explanatory paragraph (or paragraphs) is written like a long-form sales pitch. What I mean is, as the client reads the explanatory paragraphs on my website, I am inviting them into a story in which they play the hero struggling with a problem, who then uses my products and services to solve their problem.

The example paragraph I recommend uses *The Customer Is the Hero Sales Framework*, a framework I will teach you in the next chapter.

That said, here is what the explanatory paragraphs on your website could look like:

> ## It's Hard Enough to Build a Business. You **Don't** Have to Build It Alone.
>
> Building a business is hard. You need to get your mission right, then your marketing message, then your sales pitch, then your products, then your management and operations, and finally your cash flow management. Very few small business owners understand how to operate the six necessary pillars of a strong business and that's why most small businesses fail.
>
> Schedule your intake call today and let's get started building the small business of your dreams. To schedule your intake call, simply click below.
>
> **Schedule a Discovery Call**

Notes on the Explanatory Paragraph Section

When your explanatory paragraph uses *The Customer Is the Hero Sales Framework*, it doesn't have to be long. Even as your future client reads this section of your website, the light bulbs will turn on and they will finally start to see that this is an opportunity they can't pass up.

SECTION SEVEN: YOUR LEAD GENERATOR

If you've included the six sections of a coach's landing page I've described above, you will likely close several clients. However, there are still many clients who want more information or who need a longer runway to get comfortable with the idea of hiring a coach. We don't want to lose a client just because they aren't ready to hire you immediately. For those future clients, we are going to include a follow-up strategy that will help us stay in touch and continue to build more familiarity and trust.

Most future clients won't opt in to your newsletter or give you their email address so you can "keep in touch." Instead, they will only give you their email address in exchange for something of value.

The next section you will want to include on your website is an ad for your lead generator. Not only will you want an ad for your lead generator on your website, but you will want an exit-intent pop-up ad for your lead generator as well. I will show you examples of good lead generators in the next chapter. For now, though, know that the purpose of the lead generator is to gather email addresses so you can follow up with potential clients and continue to earn their trust.

Take My 12-Minute Assessment and Get a Custom Plan To **Grow Your Business**

Did you know your small business has six parts and each of those parts must be strong in order for your business to grow?

What kind of shape is your business in? Click below to find out.

Take the Assessment

You will find, over time, a slight majority of your clients will sign on for your coaching because they received emails from you. In other words, more than 50 percent of your future business depends on you creating a lead generator and following up with weekly (at the very least) automated emails for an extended period of time.

Notes on Your Lead Generator

You can actually use several lead generators at the same time as a way of qualifying different segments of clients. Your options for lead generators are virtually limitless. As with all the sections of this website, customize your lead generator to best fit the kind of coaching you intend to offer.

■

If you create a coaching website with the sections I've shown you, your coaching business will grow.

Your website can certainly include more sections than the ones I've included here—but these sections are the ones I believe are nonnegotiable. They are also the only sections most coaches actually need. If you create a website using these seven sections, your coaching business will grow.

In the next chapter, I will give you some lead generator ideas and also share sample emails you can send to potential clients once they visit your website. When you stay in touch with potential clients via email, you will move them further and further past the curiosity and enlightenment phases of a relationship into a willingness to make a commitment and engage you as a coach.

STEP THREE   93

Again, the main benefit of creating a website for your coaching services is to help clients move further into the journey of hiring you and having their lives changed by your coaching services. But that isn't the only benefit.

> As you wireframe your website, you will also be clarifying your offer so that *you* better understand your value as a coach.

The process of wireframing your website may prove to be transformative for you. Before you wireframe your website you may not fully believe in yourself or your services, but as you build your sales pitch in the form of a website, you will find yourself more fully believing in yourself and what you offer. Make sure to follow through with this step in the playbook.

■

Again, if you want to see examples of twenty-seven effective coaching websites from coaches who are succeeding in their various fields (not just business coaching), visit CoachBuilder.com.

STEP FOUR

Learn to Write Great Emails That Close the Deal

fter you know what products you are going to offer, have a list of potential customers, and have clarified your offer in the form of a website, you'll want to follow up with leads using simple, automated emails that nurture the new relationships you're building with potential clients.

The reason you will want to nurture these new business relationships through an automated email campaign is because hiring a coach is not an impulse decision. And because it's not an impulse decision, you'll want to earn trust with potential clients over a long period of time.

> People tend to buy products and services from brands and leaders they feel are familiar, and familiarity doesn't happen fast.

What is the formula for earning trust? It's this: value over time.

The best way to move a large group of future clients through the three stages of relationship—that is curiosity, enlightenment, and commitment—is to acquire their email address and send them emails over six to twelve—or as long as fifty-two—consecutive weeks.

Another reason to stay in touch with potential clients over an extended period of time is because coaching clients do not tend to hire a coach because they were sold on the idea of hiring a coach. They tend to hire a coach because they entered a window in which their problems and frustrations triggered them to make the decision to hire a coach. And that only happens if you've stayed in touch with them long enough to extend familiarity into their buying zone.

> The key to growing your coaching business, then, is to make sure potential clients are familiar with you and the coaching products you offer during the time window in which they are experiencing a business challenge.

If a potential client inquires about your service and you don't continue to send them emails reminding them you exist long after they make their first encounter with you, there is a significant chance they will have forgotten you a short time later when they encounter a business challenge. Nothing, and I repeat, *nothing*, will grow your coaching business faster than staying in touch with potential clients before and especially during an experience of frustration on their part.

The main reason to create an automated email campaign is not to sell future clients on your service, but to extend the enlightenment phase of the customer journey long enough that it will cover the window of frustration your coaching clients are bound to pass through. You will find, as your lead generator collects email addresses and your automated emails extend the window of enlightenment, the appreciation for your wisdom as a coach grows and the result is you sell more of your coaching products.

USE A LEAD GENERATOR SO POTENTIAL CLIENTS CAN TAKE A SAFE NEXT STEP

The best way to secure email addresses is not to simply ask for them, though this is critical. It's to ask for an email address in exchange for a valuable insight. In marketing speak we often call these valuable insights lead generators. Creating a lead generator and sending out subsequent emails that fuel word of mouth will make growing your coaching business much easier.

The coaches I've worked with who have created lead generators followed by automated follow-up emails have grown their coaching businesses much faster than those who do not. And while it may seem intimidating to try to create some sort of lead generator and sign your name to it, it's not all that difficult.

I built my initial business with a lead generator called "Five Things Your Website Should Include," and built it even larger with a video series called "Five-Minute Marketing Makeover." Since then, I've created dozens of lead generators, including PDFs, podcasts, webinars, live events, and minicourses. Without question, my business was built on the power of lead generators and follow-up emails and your business growth can be generated through similar strategies.

That said, what sort of lead generator should you create?

It depends. You want your lead generator to do two things: **qualify potential clients** and **create trust and familiarity**.

Who is your perfect client? It's the client you enjoy working with and can get the best results for. As it relates to business coaching, some coaches are terrific at helping their clients create their marketing plan and execute that plan. Other coaches are great at helping their clients know how to find new sources of revenue and establish strong and healthy cash flow. Others are great at launching products or managing a leadership transition. You may even specialize in helping small business owners prepare to sell their companies.

When it comes to creating a lead generator, the question you want to ask is, "What is the main problem I want to help my clients resolve?" Once you answer that question, you will want to create a lead generator that attracts clients who are struggling with that specific problem.

For instance, if you are wanting to work with clients who are challenged with internal tension on their leadership team, you might create a lead generator called "The Perfect Leadership Team: The Three Essential Roles Necessary to Manage Any Small Business."

> Lead generators are sometimes called "lead magnets" because they are designed to attract the kinds of leads you want to work with.

Many coaches use a simple assessment to attract leads. After sending a potential client to the assessment, the coach engages the future client in a phone call and reviews that client's custom report, encouraging the client and also pointing out the areas of weakness in the client's business that, of course, they can provide coaching products to strengthen.

Even if the client declines the invitation to engage the coach's services after taking the assessment and engaging the coach in a review session, the client continues to get emails over the next six to fifty-two weeks that result in a surprising number of decisions to come back and engage the coach and purchase one of their coaching products. Again, clients tend to make purchases when they encounter a challenge, not when they are being sold the service itself.

In our experience helping coaches build their coaching businesses, we've found that without the lead generator, follow-up call, and subsequent email campaign, many coaches would only receive half the orders they currently enjoy. The lead generator and subsequent nurture emails are that important.

I know creating a lead generator and subsequent email campaign sounds like a lot of work, but the work is worth it. Imagine spending a couple of weeks creating a lead generator and ten or twelve nurture emails and then enjoying the dozens of clients they help you close each year, year after year.

To get started, think small. Don't try to start with a free on-demand course. Instead, start with a text-based PDF that offers to solve a problem only your qualified clients might be struggling with.

Here are a few types of simple, text-based lead generators you can easily create:

1. **The Checklist:** Create a checklist that helps your future clients better understand what it is they need to do to solve a problem. For example, "How to Run Your Small Business with Only Five Meetings per Week" or "The Small Business Cash Flow

Road Map—How to Never Run Out of Money
Again."

2. **The Worksheet:** Giving potential clients a tool they
   can use to solve a problem will earn their trust and
   position you as an expert. Worksheets such as "The
   Perfect Week Template" or "The Tag Line Creation
   Worksheet" will either position you as a productivity
   coach or a marketing expert and attract the kinds of
   clients you hope to work with.

3. **The Assessment:** If there are ten or twenty questions
   you can ask that will help future clients understand
   the nature of their problem, you can create an
   assessment in which they thoughtfully consider their
   challenges and then realize how much they need your
   coaching.

4. **The Interview:** If there is an aspirational leader in
   your future client's field of expertise, consider getting
   in touch with them for an interview and then offering
   that interview as a lead generator. Interviewing a
   popular head football coach about how to build and
   manage a team or even a popular artist about how she
   manages work-life balance will attract the kinds of
   clients who consider that person an aspirational
   figure. People will give up their email address to hear
   from their heroes.

5. **A Solution Article:** If you have a solution to a
   problem your clients struggle with, for example, a
   small business tax strategy, you can write an article

called "Ten Reasons You're Paying Too Much in
Taxes." The article could talk about the tax code and
then offer a strategy to lower the client's tax exposure.
The point of a solution article is to introduce a
solution that will require your help to fully execute. If
your client is struggling with a problem, they will be
more likely to download your article, and then, if they
want you to walk them through the solution rather
than just read about it, they will be more likely to hire
you as a coach.

Coaches sometimes ask me how much value they should give
away in their lead generators. The truth is, it varies. I like to give
away a considerable amount of help for free because it creates
reciprocity, but the general rule is this: Give away the *why* but sell
the *how*. For instance, you might give away the "why" of your tax
strategies—that there are people paying far less taxes than others
because they know something other people don't—but then sell
the actual information on how people pay less in taxes through a
coaching small group, workshop, keynote, or one-on-one coaching sessions.

The list of possibilities for your lead generators is endless. Ten
minutes of thoughtful reflection in a coffee shop will net you
several ideas. Better, talking to potential clients or doing some
research into their frustrations will net even more ideas.

Generating qualified leads is critical to growing your coaching
business. If your lead generator attracts the right clients and ten
people give you their email address, you know you have ten qualified leads. And remember this: Every follow-up email you send
after they download your lead generator guides your future client

further through the enlightenment phase and closer to the commitment phase.

CLOSE MORE SALES WITH EFFECTIVE EMAILS

After a lead gives you their email address, you will want to follow up over the next six weeks to one year with strong, valuable emails. And remember, the longer you extend the window in which you stay in touch, the more likely that window will overlap with a challenge your future client experiences.

What sorts of emails should you send out in an automated nurture campaign? As a general rule, you will want to use *The Customer Is the Hero Sales Framework* to write your emails. I created the formula years ago as part of a sales training curriculum and it turned out to be so valuable that it's all I teach anymore when it comes to sales. The formula itself can be used in emails, elevator pitches, keynotes, webinars, proposals, and even to create talking points for casual sales conversations.

After you learn the framework, you can create dozens of emails that engage clients where they are and position you as an expert who can help solve your clients' problems.

Let's take a closer look at *The Customer Is the Hero Sales Framework* so we can better understand how and why it works so well to nurture clients and build trust.

THE CUSTOMER IS THE HERO
SALES FRAMEWORK

To create emails that win, structure your emails using this formula:

Step One: Start with the problem. Describe the main problem your coaching service solves. Of course, you may solve many problems but you'll want to choose an overarching problem that will attract qualified leads for the product you want to focus on most. For example, a good problem to talk about if you want to sell more of your fractional COO services might be: Small business owners often *feel like their people are wearing too many hats and nobody knows what their real job description is.*

Again, if you define the problem you solve, potential clients will "find themselves" and will feel like you're reading their journal. Describe the problem well and potential clients will be more likely to lean in and desire to know more about you and your coaching services.

Step Two: Position your product as the solution to your customer's problem. Now that you've defined what problem you can help your client solve, you will want to position your coaching service (or at least one of the products within your menu of coaching services) as the solution to that problem. If you want to coach small business owners, you will want to let them know about the six-month small group you offer that helps them double their revenue. If you're helping them position their small business to sell, explain how your "Sell Your Business" package can walk them through the preparation process. The rule is this: For whatever problem you define in the first paragraph, position yourself or one of your coaching products as the solution in the second paragraph.

The reason the two parts of *The Customer Is the Hero Sales Framework* are effective is because all human behavior is motivated by the opening and closing of a story loop. A story loop is essentially a question or a sort of riddle that the audience pays attention to because they want to solve that problem or riddle. For instance, will the hero rescue the victim? Will the team win the championship? Will the couple resolve their challenges and get married? If you open a good story loop, the audience will pay attention until you close that loop. How does this relate to growing your coaching business? Simple. If you open the story loop of a chaotic management system, your client will have to buy your product and hire you as a fractional COO to close that story loop and organize their team. The first two steps of *The Customer Is the Hero Sales Framework*, then, are to open a story loop by talking about your customer's problem and then offer to close that story loop when and if they buy your product.

Step Three: Build a bridge from the customer's problem to your solution. You've already included a visual, three-step plan on your website, but repeat it again in a separate paragraph in your emails. Again, the purpose of the plan is to give your potential clients a few baby steps they can take that will propel them from their problem to your solution. Give the potential client a small, safe, easy first step to take and they will be more likely to start walking toward you.

STEP FOUR   105

Step Four: Paint the negative stakes. A good story includes positive and negative stakes. Something must be won or lost based
on whether the hero accomplishes the task at hand. Why? Because
if there are no stakes, there is no story. What this means for you
and your coaching business is that if nothing can be won or lost
by hiring or not hiring you as a coach, nobody will feel a sense of
urgency about hiring you. Stakes make a story interesting. If the
hero does not disarm the bomb, many people will be hurt. Or if
the athlete does not perform at their best, the season will be lost.
Stakes in a story create a strong sense of urgency and so stakes
should be included in your email copy. In the next two sections of
your email, you'll paint the stakes. Start with the negative stakes.
Will your potential client lose ground to the competition if they
do not hire you? Is there a chance they could go under if they
don't engage the solution you are proposing? Will your client be
passed over for the promotion if they don't hire you as a career
coach? Let the customer know what the stakes of *not* hiring you
are in this fourth paragraph.

Step Five: Paint the positive stakes. A good story involves a hero
who is always vacillating between the negative and positive stakes.
Suspense, intrigue, and engagement all increase when the stakes
are made clear. After your future client reads about the negative
stakes, offer them a vision of what their lives could look like if
they avoid a potentially dark fate. If you want to invite your customer into an exciting story, let them know about the terrific,
amazing reality they could experience if they hire you as a coach.
Why is this important? Because all stories foreshadow a climactic
scene in which the good guy defeats the bad guy in order to win
the day. When you foreshadow a climactic scene in your future

customer's life, they will be much more inclined to engage your services.

Step Six: Call the customer to action. Lastly, you will call your customer to action. Why must you ask your client to make a purchase? Because an astounding number of potential clients will not take action unless you challenge them to do so. At this point in the email, your reader will likely want to take that first baby step, but they aren't going to do so unless you challenge them. If your first baby step is to schedule an intake session, spell that request out clearly as you close your email by saying something like this: *I have made room on my schedule to talk to small business owners about these challenges every Monday. To schedule thirty minutes with me, simply click on this link.*

■

The Customer Is the Hero Sales Framework makes it much easier to write emails that are compelling and effective. Using these six paragraphs as a guide, you will create winning sales pitches in every single email you send.

Below, I've printed examples of sales emails you can send (after you edit them to fit your voice and coaching parameters) that will grow your coaching business.

The way an email campaign can work for your coaching business is simple. Start by sending about seven sales emails. These emails are direct and to the point, essentially asking potential clients to purchase your coaching services. If they do not purchase one of your products, however, you still want to keep in touch with them by switching to a nurture campaign. Nurture emails are emails that offer free value but don't try too hard to sell the reader anything. Essentially, nurture emails are simply emails that continue to build familiarity and trust and extend the buying window for weeks or months to come.

Here are seven sales emails you can send to clients after they download your lead generator or after you've met them in person:

EMAIL #1:
THE "GOOD TO MEET YOU" EMAIL

This email will help you:

- Honor the fact that the story is not about you; it's about the potential client.

- Show them you were truly listening when you first met, thus further positioning you as the guide and further earning their trust.

- Invite the customer into a story in which they use your product or service to solve their problem, thus growing their small business and your coaching business at the same time.

Whether you've encountered a client in person or if they've downloaded your lead generator, this email will be an effective next point of contact. I've written this email from the perspective of a coach who has met a client in person, but the first sentence or two can be edited to fit an automated system in which a future client has downloaded a lead generator.

Sample Email

■ **TOM,**

Thanks for taking the time to meet yesterday. As we talked, it sounded like you were having serious cash flow challenges. You aren't alone. The good news is the only people who struggle with cash flow management are the people who are capable of building a company that brings in cash.

In other words, the problem is a problem of success. That said, growth requires investment, which often leads to cash flow issues.

Because money is a difficult thing to manage, it's important to separate money into several different accounts so that you have clear optics on where you stand financially.

I coach my clients through a system called "Small Business Cash Flow Made Simple" that divides your incoming and outgoing money into five different checking accounts.

I've yet to coach a client through the process who hasn't gained peace of mind after getting the clarity (and hope) they needed surrounding their finances.

I can coach you through this process alone, or I can include you in a six-month small group with other small business owners in which we tackle the cash flow playbook along with five other playbooks that will help you grow your small business. In the small group, we overhaul your business in six simple steps, each step taking about a month to implement. Cash flow will be included.

The way I work with clients is to identify their most pressing problems, customize a plan to help them solve those problems, and then establish a series of meetings in which we implement the solutions. It's all pretty simple.

> The bottom line is there is no reason you shouldn't have
> extreme clarity about your finances. When we work together, it will
> be easy for you to implement a solution and start getting a great
> night's sleep again.
>
> If you have time on Monday, I can jump on a Zoom call at
> 9:00 a.m. to talk through whether or not we want to work together.
> Otherwise I can work with your assistant to get us on a call soon.
>
> Sincerely,
>
> **CAITLYN SMITH**
>
> Caitlyn Small Business Coaching

A good follow-up email does a few important things. First, it recalls the initial conversation you had (or the fact that they were interested in your lead generator) as a way of telling them you are paying attention to *their* needs. The email should demonstrate empathy and authority—that is, that you understand and care about their problems and also that you have what it takes to help them solve that problem.

> The one-two punch of empathy and authority positions
> you as a guide in your future client's life.

Second, the email pinpoints the problem your future client mentioned in your conversation and brings their problem back to the forefront, helping to make the problem something they will want to solve sooner rather than later.

After empathizing with your customer's problem, the email positions your products as a viable solution. The email also spells out a three-step plan, paints the positive and negative stakes, asks for the order, and calls the customer to action by recommending a next step.

As you can see, the email above simply but faithfully follows *The Customer Is the Hero Sales Framework* and so it's clear, interesting, and will motivate action.

If every potential client you speak with received an email like the one above, a decent percentage of those potential clients would take the first baby step of taking an assessment. After taking the assessment, plenty would sign up for your coaching, especially if your menu of coaching products were defined clearly on your website.

Again, the email above is great to send to clients after you've met them in person. While it can easily be edited for the purpose of an automated follow-up after somebody downloads your lead generator, I'll devote the next six sample emails in this chapter specifically to automated follow-ups. Of course, you will want to edit these emails to reflect the kind of coaching you intend to offer, but my hope is these emails will help you understand the tone and intent you will want to communicate to attract and close more clients.

Each of the sample emails below helps the coach sell a product called "Small Business Community Group." As you read through the emails, notice how the coach sets up the product as a solution to the customer's problem, paints the stake, includes a plan, and calls the customer to action. As you think about selling your coaching products, you will want to use the same methods.

With that, here are six sample emails you can use as inspiration to create your own campaign to be sent after a client downloads your lead generator:

EMAIL #2: THE "THANK-YOU AND CLARIFICATION OF OFFER" EMAIL

This email will help you:

- Define the problems you solve.

- Clarify the products you offer.

- Begin to close the deal.

Sample Email

■ **DEAR NAME,**

Thank you for downloading the *Small Business Growth Plan Checklist*. The checklist is designed to help you organize your business, align your priorities, market and sell your products, and even manage your cash flow. If you're struggling in any of these areas, I'm here to help.

It's nearly impossible to grow a business without following a plan. The truth is, though, most small business owners don't have a plan. That's probably why 65 percent of small businesses fail.

I've enjoyed helping dozens of small business owners like you grow their businesses. I do that through a small group called a Small Business Community Group in which we optimize your small business for revenue and profit. The goal of my Small Business Community Group is simple: double your revenue.

We do this by rewriting your mission statement, clarifying your marketing message, overhauling your sales process, optimizing your product offering, streamlining your overhead and operations, and finally introducing you to an easy and effective way to manage your cash flow.

Signing up for my Small Business Community Group is easy. Simply respond to this email, let me know you'd like to meet, and I'll organize a time for us to jump on a Zoom call. If we both agree a Small Business Community Group is a good fit for you, I'll make room in my next cohort. Once you join a community group you will get weekly inspiration and practical advice you can use to see a massive impact on your bottom line. Plus, you will be able to interact with other small business owners just like you so you feel less alone as you grow your small business. All of this translates into no more restless nights wondering if you're going to be one of the small businesses that fail.

You really don't have to build your small business alone. You can join a mastermind of other small business owners who are all interested in one thing: growing their small businesses.

Again, if you'd like to jump on a Zoom call, simply reply to this email or click HERE to schedule an appointment with me. I'd love to talk about how we're helping businesses like yours execute a growth plan that works.

Sincerely,

JIM SPENCER
Jim Spencer Coaching

EMAIL #3:
THE "EMPATHY AND COMPETENCY" EMAIL

This email will help you:

- Share your specific origin story (you will customize this for yourself, of course).

- Position yourself as the guide.

- Earn respect from your future client.

- Help your future client picture themselves experiencing the success you have experienced.

Sample Email

■ **DEAR NAME,**

Many years ago I owned and operated a small business. I say "owned" and "operated" but, truly, it never looked like I was fully operating anything. I felt trapped inside a machine of my own making.

I owned a car wash business, or, rather, a car wash business owned me. I had three locations and spent all my time driving back and forth to make sure the machinery was working and our teams had actually shown up to wash the cars. It was organized chaos, at best.

It wasn't until I discovered a smooth process for running a small business that things began to change. The process helped me organize the six parts of my business so it could manage itself and I could sit back and make money.

I sold that business five years ago and seriously considered retiring. After I sold my business, though, I found myself coaching other small business owners to grow their own businesses and discovered I enjoyed the work. So now I'm a business coach. And I love it.

I've been able to help all kinds of businesses professionalize their operations and grow. I've worked with every kind of business you can imagine, from dog walking to real estate to pizza restaurants. It turns out every business needs the exact same process I discovered years ago.

If you're feeling overwhelmed, I'd like to help. Your business can operate reliably and predictably.

I have a Small Business Community Group starting soon but am also available for individual coaching. I'd love to fit you into my schedule. If you're in need of a business coach, schedule a Zoom call with me HERE.

Here's to the success of your small business,

JIM SPENCER
Jim Spencer Coaching

EMAIL #4: THE "TESTIMONY AND CALL TO ACTION" EMAIL

This email will help you:

- Create social proof.

- Generate a sense of urgency.

- Continue to clarify your offer.

Sample Email

■ **DEAR NAME,**

> My next Small Business Community Group is starting up soon. I'm making room for ten small business owners and we will almost certainly fill up.
>
> As a small business owner, you likely get very few opportunities to talk to other small business owners. Few people in your family or immediate community are dealing with the problems you face every day.
>
> During the six months you will spend in our Small Business Community Group, you will be able to talk openly about the unique challenges you experience and, almost certainly, will hear from other small business owners who have solved the exact same problems. Not to mention the six frameworks we will be learning will help you solve foundational problems in leadership, marketing, sales, product optimization, management, and cash flow.
>
> If you're feeling alone and want to grow your small business, let's talk about getting you into the next small group.

John Gerber joined my Small Business Community Group last year and listen to what he had to say:

"My revenue has increased by 57 percent after being in Jim's Small Business Community Group. But that's not the best part. The best part is the friendships I've taken away from the six months we spent together. Joining the Small Business Community Group with Jim was the best decision I've ever made for my business."

If John's results sound good to you, schedule a Zoom call with me HERE and I'll get you signed up.

I look forward to helping you organize and grow your small business.

Talk soon,

JIM SPENCER

Jim Spencer Coaching

EMAIL #5:
THE "OVERCOME OBJECTION" EMAIL

This email will help you:

- Overcome your client's buying objections.

- Give your client a vision of their potential.

- Further define the value you offer.

Sample Email

■ **DEAR NAME,**

The number one reason small business owners DON'T join a Small Business Community Group is they feel like they don't have time for the commitment. But not having time to work on your business, or for that matter be present with family, enjoy a hobby, or even get together with friends, is the very problem our Small Business Community Groups solve.

When a business is organized and operating the way it is supposed to, the owner of the business will have plenty of margin to rest, dream, and be inspired. Many of us need to figure out how to OWN our business rather than MANAGE our business.

My Small Business Community Group is an ongoing community group in which you share your challenges, exchange best practices, receive support and inspiration, and talk about how to optimize your business for revenue and profit.

If you want your time back, join my Small Business Community Group. All you need to do is click HERE and schedule a Zoom call. From there, I will get you signed up so you can start meeting with a community and overhauling your small business today.

Let's get your time back.

Schedule a Zoom call HERE and let's get you your time back!

Talk soon,

JIM SPENCER

Jim Spencer Coaching

EMAIL #6:
THE "TIME IS RUNNING OUT" EMAIL

This email will help you:

- Generate even more urgency.

- Close the sale.

- Force the reader to make a decision.

Sample Email

■ **DEAR NAME,**

Time is running out to join my next Small Business Community Group.

Our first meeting is coming up.

If you aren't part of a small business community, consider joining us. When you have a group of small business owners to talk to, you solve problems faster, realize growth opportunities more easily, shave hours off your workweek, get better sleep because you are less stressed, and your small business begins to grow again.

If you have questions, I can answer any of them on a Zoom call. Just respond to this email saying you'd like to get together and I'll make the rest happen.

If you don't sign up soon, I won't be offering another small group for at least six months. That means you'll miss out on six months' worth of growth opportunity.

To schedule a quick Zoom call so I can share the dates with you, just click HERE.

Remember, you only have a few more days to sign up. Let's get together and talk soon.

Sincerely,

JIM SPENCER

Jim Spencer Coaching

EMAIL #7:
THE "FINAL REMINDER" EMAIL

This email will help you:

- Close the sale.

- Generate a final sense of urgency.

Sample Email

■ **DEAR NAME,**

Today is the last day to join my Small Business Community Group. If you want to join a group of small business owners who are growing their businesses together, click HERE and schedule a fast Zoom call.

In just a few weeks, you will have an entirely new set of friends, a growth plan for your business, and, more than anything else: HOPE. You will have hope your business can feel like a gift rather than a burden.

If you can jump on a Zoom call, you won't be left behind. Our first meeting is coming up soon.

Again, if you want to join our small group, click HERE and I'll get you set up.

Here's to the growth of your business!

JIM SPENCER
Business Made Simple Certified Coach

■

These six emails are, of course, designed to define and sell a specific product: Small Business Community Groups. As you build your own coaching business, your flagship product may differ. Regardless, you will want to write at least six emails like this to on-ramp potential customers to your flagship product or service. You will be surprised at how many people get back in touch with you after receiving the fourth or fifth email. Why will it take so long? Because joining a community group is not an impulse decision. People often need a month or two to consider the idea before it starts making sense to them. And if you continue emailing them while they are considering joining you, they will be much more likely to see that fifth or sixth email and schedule a Zoom call. However, if you go silent on them, they will forget your offer.

CONTINUE EMAILING YOUR POTENTIAL CLIENTS FOR WEEKS, MONTHS, AND EVEN YEARS TO COME

After you send your first six sales emails, you can use your CRM to put future clients in what we call a "nurture track." The nurture track is a series of emails that go out each week and share useful content with potential clients.

The idea behind the nurture track is to continue to remind clients you exist and to remind them about the kinds of problems you can help them resolve. The reason you can slow your email release to twice each month for the nurture track is because the goal is simply to stay in touch and continue to build trust.

Even if a client rejects the offer to join your flagship small group, you'll want to continue sending emails for weeks, months, and even years to come. The longer potential clients receive emails from you, the more familiar they will be with you and the more likely they will be to eventually purchase your products and services.

Unlike the sample sales emails I showed you earlier, nurture emails are not really trying to close a deal; they simply exist to be helpful and to remind as many people as possible that you are a coach and you can be called if they get into trouble.

Again, the reason these emails are so important is because clients do not tend to invest in coaching on impulse. Instead, they invest in coaching only when they are experiencing challenges. The longer you send a potential client emails, the more likely one of your emails will overlap with a problem they are currently experiencing.

> Why send so many nurture emails? Because if you don't
> keep a hook in the water, you will never catch a fish.

Every year I join a group of about ten friends to fly-fish in Montana. Those days on the river are some of my favorites, year after year. To be honest, none of us are great fly fisherman but I have picked up on some strategies that increase my fish count. The number one predictor of fish being caught, however, has little to do with the fly I use or the placement of said fly. The guys who catch the most fish all have one thing in common: They keep their flies on the water all day. What I mean is, they don't sit back in the boat and drink a beer or spend hours untangling their lines. They stand and cast and then cast again, racking up the minutes and hours their fly is looking attractive to the fish swimming just beneath the surface. The more time their fly is on the water, the more fish they catch.

Building your coaching business works the same way. Every email is a cast of the fly, and the more nurture emails you create, the more time your fly sits on the water. Do the emails need to be good? It helps, for sure. But the reality is, the number one predictor of whether or not you will grow your coaching business is whether or not you continue to send emails after the other coaches have stopped.

The point here is this: The more, and the longer, you remind customers you exist, the more likely they will be to place an eventual order. This is true in coaching just as it's true in every other kind of business.

WHAT KINDS OF NURTURE EMAILS SHOULD WE SEND OUT IN AN EFFORT TO STAY FAMILIAR IN A CUSTOMER'S MIND?

When you switch to a nurture campaign (after the sales campaign runs its course) you will want every email to offer value. The best way you can do this is to make sure every email explains a little bit about how to solve a problem. Why offer such terrific free value? Because, again, trust is built by offering value over time. And nobody is going to hire you unless they trust you.

Even though nurture emails offer free value, you will still want to talk about the products you sell. The difference between a sales email and a nurture email, however, is that a nurture email also includes a teaching component. Whether or not the recipient of your nurture emails makes a purchase from you, they will still get great value, thus positioning you as a coach in their lives and also creating a sense of reciprocity.

Here is a list of the kinds of "nurture" emails you can send that will enlighten your clients, earn trust, and encourage them to commit:

1. **The Problem/Solution Email:** This email will define a specific business problem your clients are dealing with and then detail exactly how to solve that problem.

2. **The "Here's How They Did It" Email:** Send potential clients a case study and testimonial from an existing client who has experienced success from your coaching. Detail how they solved a specific problem using your coaching advice or frameworks.

3. The "Step-by-Step" Email: Are there five or six steps a person can take to solve a specific business problem? If so, detail those steps in this email.

4. The "Introduction to an Expert" Email: Did you read an article recently that you think would help your potential clients? If so, summarize the advice the expert gave and include a link to that article.

5. The Sales Email: Just like in the sales email I showed you earlier, in this email you are going to explain the products you offer and ask potential clients to schedule an intake call so they can find out which of your coaching products are best for them. This is a commitment email and you will want to place these emails in the sequence every three or four emails.

These five kinds of emails, sent out at a cadence of one email per week, followed by the same theme-driven emails sent in the same order for several more months, will grow your coaching business. Notice the fifth email is another straight sales email. Why include a sales email in a nurture campaign? Even though (as you will see) every nurture email still has a sales component to it, occasionally you will want to send a strong sales email that encourages your future clients to place an order.

The point is this: When you create a sales campaign followed by a nurture campaign, more and more potential clients will begin to think of you as a go-to source for help. And a percentage of the recipients of these emails will hire you. The more email addresses you get, and the longer you send emails to those recipients, the more likely you will be to engage paying clients in both your flagship product and beyond.

Here are five sample nurture emails you can use to build your coaching business. Each email is only a sample of the sort of email you can create within that theme. You can create an endless variety of each email. To be sure, these are not the only kinds of emails you can send but these five emails should be effective for you.

NURTURE EMAIL #1:
THE PROBLEM/SOLUTION EMAIL

Sample Email

SUBJECT: 5 Meetings You Need to Manage Your Small Business

■ **DEAR NAME,**

When you grew your business past $1 million in annual revenue, you likely noticed something. You noticed that you were spending less and less time on the things that used to make you money and more and more time dealing with the drama that comes from working with a team.

What do I mean by drama? I mean hiring, firing, dealing with office conflict, making sure you've got the right people in the right seats, and trying to develop members of your team so they perform their jobs well.

Paying more attention to your team than you do to your products or customers, though, can lead to trouble. If you aren't careful, your sales will begin to slow and the quality of the service you offer may decline as well.

In order to succeed, your business needs you doing what you do best, whether that's creating products, interacting with customers, or closing sales.

But how can you get back to your sweet spot?

The key is to install a management and operations system that makes sure your business works like a machine.

This fall, my Small Business Community Group will be focusing exclusively on management and operations. We are going to learn how to run our small businesses using just five meetings. I'd love for you to join us.

Here are the specific meetings you will want to install in order to manage your team (and your time) well:

1. **The All-Staff Meeting:** This meeting is exactly what it sounds like, a meeting in which you and your entire team review the goals of the company. This meeting takes place once each week.

2. **The Leadership Meeting:** Right after your All-Staff Meeting, sit with your leadership team and tackle any open projects that need action. This meeting also happens once each week.

3. **The Department Stand-Up:** Each department inside your small business needs a fast, fifteen-minute stand-up every day so that every member of your team knows what's expected of them each day.

4. **The Personal Priority Speed Check:** Once each week, each member of your team should meet with their department head as a way of clarifying what's expected of them personally.

5. **The Quarterly Performance Review:** Each quarter every member of your team will meet with their supervisor to address performance. This meeting lasts about thirty minutes. Your team is desperate for feedback and coaching and this meeting is where they get it.

If you'd like to know more about these meetings then join my Small Business Community Group. Taking part in my Small Business Community Group is simple. First, let's jump on a Zoom call so I can better understand where you're struggling. Second, jump into a couple of our meetings and then, if you like the community, join us every month for as long as you need us.

If you're dealing with the problem of managing your people, our management and operations focus is going to help.

None of us signed up to manage chaos. What we need is a system that sets us free to do what we love and make a profit in the process.

Click HERE to schedule that Zoom call. I look forward to talking soon.

JAMES THATCHER
Thatcher Coaching Group

NURTURE EMAIL #2:
THE "HERE'S HOW THEY DID IT" EMAIL

Sample Email

■ **DEAR NAME,**

Marcus didn't come to me because his business was struggling. In fact, he was in the middle of his best revenue year yet. The reason he came to me is because he felt trapped. To Marcus, his business had become a prison.

How was he trapped? In order to make payroll every month, he had to do most of the work. Even though he had a marketing team, he had to come up with all the ideas and do all the research. Not only this, he had to call his primary clients to close the deal. He also had to make sure his inventory was in stock and that his products were created with the same level of quality his customers had come to expect.

The bigger his business got, the more Marcus felt trapped.

When Marcus joined our Small Business Community Group, he was beside himself. Actually, he hardly had any time to be in the room and wondered whether he had made a mistake. But after our first meeting, Marcus realized he wasn't alone. And he realized there was help.

There is no challenge you or Marcus are currently experiencing that a small business owner hasn't already dealt with and conquered. You just aren't in the room when the solution is being discussed.

What's the solution? It can vary based on your specific situation, but here is a basic playbook for owning rather than managing your small business:

First, create systems and processes that allow your business to run like a machine.

Second, install those systems and processes into a daily, weekly, monthly, and annual calendar.

Third, now that you've built a machine, hire an operator to run your machine. Be careful, though, because your operator needs to be wired a specific way in order to succeed.

If all of this sounds like a journey you need to take, I'd love to explain it further. You can schedule a Zoom call with me HERE to talk about how you can transform your business into a productive and profitable machine.

For now, though, know that there is hope. If you create the systems and processes, place them into a calendar to keep yourself accountable, and then hire somebody good at managing a machine, you can be free. It happened for Marcus and it can happen for you.

Today, Marcus spends half his time either fishing or playing golf. No kidding. And his business has grown, not shrunk.

If you're looking for this kind of growth even as you take more time to enjoy the fruits of your labor, let's jump on a Zoom call.

Here's to the growth of your small business.

JANE SEYMORE
Small Business Coach

NURTURE EMAIL #3:
THE "STEP-BY-STEP" EMAIL

Sample Email

SUBJECT: Three steps to hiring a virtual assistant

■ **DEAR NAME,**

If you're a successful solopreneur and are thinking about hiring a small team but are a little afraid of the extra responsibility, you should consider hiring a virtual assistant as your first hire.

A virtual assistant can transform your business and your life. And while it may seem like a big step, once you take it you will wonder why you didn't make the move sooner.

Why is it such a good move? A virtual assistant can scale with you. You can start your assistant out at ten hours per week and scale all the way to forty, meaning you are not exposing yourself to a giant payroll bill every month.

Before you hire a virtual assistant, though, here are three steps you will want to take.

Step One: Make a list of all the personal and professional tasks that take up the majority of your time. Make sure to include personal tasks like scheduling haircuts, booking dinner reservations, planning vacations, and so on. As a solopreneur, the business needs your time, and the less you're bogged down in tasks, the more time you have to grow your business. Do not differentiate between your business tasks and your personal tasks. Your virtual assistant is on the team to serve you because you are the business.

Step Two: Create a perfect week for your virtual assistant. Before you hire an assistant, you should know what they will be working on. You don't want them to step into chaos, so sit down and write down the repeating tasks they will do each week. This will be an encouraging exercise for you because you will quickly realize how much time you will gain with their help. Their perfect week, in other words, will free you up to have your perfect week.

Step Three: Make the call and get going. There are many virtual assistant companies out there but I like BELAY Solutions. I've sent plenty of clients to them and they do a great job taking care of each of my clients' needs. Once you are paired with the right virtual assistant, begin allowing them to manage your schedule and get that perfect week rolling.

If you take the three steps I've outlined above, you will have no problem making and employing your first hire.

As always, if you want to get on a Zoom call and talk about your current challenges, let me know. I enjoy coaching small business owners to success and can share with you how my virtual assistant and I work together to free up more of my time. You can schedule a Zoom call with me HERE.

Here's to your first hire being a life-changing experience.

To your success,

TIM PORTER

Focus Coaching Group

NURTURE EMAIL #4:
THE "INTRODUCTION TO AN EXPERT" EMAIL

Sample Email

■ **DEAR NAME,**

If you've ever felt completely hopeless about your business, or for that matter your life, you will get a great deal of hope from my friend Mignon Francois.

Mignon once lived in a small house in the Germantown neighborhood in Nashville, Tennessee. In her book, *Made from Scratch*, she tells the story of feeling trapped by an abusive husband, raising seven children on next to nothing. At her darkest moment, she nearly lost her home, her marriage, and perhaps even her life.

As her house was being foreclosed upon, though, she decided to do something about it all. She chose to start a small business and take control of her life. With $5 to her name, she went down to the grocery store and bought a box of cupcake mix. She and her children made the cupcakes and sold them. She used the profit to buy more cupcake mix and they kept going.

Today, the very house that was being foreclosed upon belongs to Mignon, long divorced from her abusive husband. The house, though, is not where Mignon lives. She lives in a much nicer place. No, the house is actually the store. Mignon has made more than $10 million selling cupcakes from two stores, one in Nashville and one in New Orleans.

If you need a little inspiration this morning, check out Mignon's story HERE.

Growing a small business is 50 percent know-how and 50 percent inspiration. If you're looking to surround yourself with inspiring people who know how to grow a small business and transform their lives, we'd love to have you in our Small Business Community Group. You can find out more about that HERE.

Growing a small business is hard, but the freedom you're hoping for might be just around the corner. Keep going. I believe in you.

Sincerely,

MICHELLE MERCED

Merced Coaching

NURTURE EMAIL #5: THE SALES EMAIL

Sample Email

- **DEAR NAME,**

The problem is, the ideas and inspiration you need to grow your business aren't going to pop into your head. Somebody actually has to put them there.

Month after month, the members of my Small Business Community Group share what's working for them to grow their small businesses, and the takeaways are incredible. When we meet, we solve each other's problems.

Not only this, but running a small business can feel so very lonely. If you're like most small business owners, you feel like the weight of the world is on your shoulders and you aren't sure how much longer you can hold it all up.

Joining our Small Business Community Group is simple. First, let's get on a Zoom call so I can better understand how your business works. Then, show up for one community group meeting. I know it can be a pain showing up in a new place with a new group of people but I believe you will find fast friends with this group. Lastly, if you like the group and want to join us, know that we'd love to include you in the community.

The answer to most of our problems can be found in community. Somebody out there has experienced your challenges and already knows how to overcome them. If you join a community of ten small business owners, you are ten times more likely to experience a breakthrough.

If you want to join my Small Business Community Group, I can explain how it all works in a Zoom call. Just schedule some time with me HERE.

Here's to your success,
CHRIS COLEMAN
Coleman Community Coaching

■

Nurture emails like these will grow your coaching business. And if you really want your coaching business to take off, start seeing yourself as a part-time marketer. If you put about five hours per week into generating, following up, and closing leads using your sales and nurture email sequences, your coaching business is sure to succeed.

START SMALL AND SCALE UP

If all of this feels overwhelming to you, start small and scale up. For example, if you don't want to create your own CRM, you can simply start by writing four or five cut-and-paste emails you can manually send to potential clients. You'll want to start with a "thanks for talking" email that expresses appreciation and then lists your services. Even this email by itself will grow your coaching business. From there, you can move on to helpful nurture emails that you send out from time to time.

In the end, however, and if you intend to grow, establishing your own CRM is going to be much more simple and enjoyable than you ever thought.

Okay, now that we've created a menu of products, generated an ongoing list of potential clients, wireframed our coaching website, and established an email sales and nurture campaign, let's create a customer journey map that will invite clients into deeper levels of coaching with us.

STEP FIVE

Map Out Your Client Journey by Creating a Marketing and Product Ladder

Your coaching business is coming together now. If you've done half of what you and I have talked about in the previous chapters, you are already running a more organized coaching business than nearly all other coaches. Most coaches are making it up as they go along. You are different. You are just as organized as you want your clients to be and because of that you will experience the kinds of results you want your clients to experience.

Let's take that level of organization a step further, now. Let's outline your client journey in the form of a marketing and product ladder.

Knowing your client journey is going to help you understand where each of your prospects and clients are on a visual ladder. As you interact with a future or existing client, you will know where they are in their relationship with you and how to guide them should they want to go further.

As I've mentioned before, all relationships move in a slow, step-by-step process. If we know what step our clients are on, we can deliver better coaching.

Another reason to create a marketing and product ladder is because by doing so you will be able to help your clients create one for their own businesses. I believe the client journey, using the simple method I will introduce you to next, is one of the best ways to help a client better service their own clients and in turn increase their revenue.

Before we get started, though, let's look again at the relationship triangle and use it to flesh out a sample ladder of our client journey.

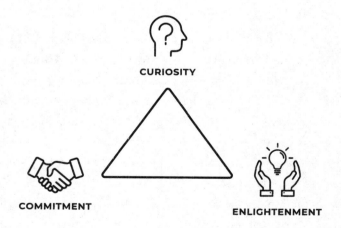

PHASE ONE: CURIOSITY

When clients first meet us, our hope is they will become curious about whether or not we can help them survive and thrive. The only thing anybody gets curious about is survival, so at the beginning of our client journey we are going to need a few tools that increase a potential client's curiosity about us and our products.

What do I mean by survival? The questions clients are asking are as simple as, *how am I going to make payroll, how am I going to save for retirement, how can I save on taxes, how can I work fewer hours but get more done?* These are the questions every business owner is asking, and if you think about it, every question has to do with their ability to survive and thrive.

The first rung of the product ladder, then, needs to address the marketing and sales collateral we will use to pique our clients' curiosity by letting them know, in short, simple sound bites, how we are going to help them survive and thrive.

For the purpose of creating a visual, let's turn all three sides of the triangle into a single ladder.

Within the three-step journey a client takes to commit to our coaching, there are baby steps in between. If you create all the marketing collateral on the next page, you will generate an enormous amount of curiosity about your coaching service, which is the goal. For certain, you do not have to create every piece of collateral I mention on the next page. Free, lead-generating, in-person events, for example, are not necessary and yet are truly helpful to pique a client's curiosity. The more things you create that pique a client's curiosity, the more people will become curious about your coaching.

By creating your client ladder you will better empathize with your clients' state and guide them more easily through the coaching experience you provide.

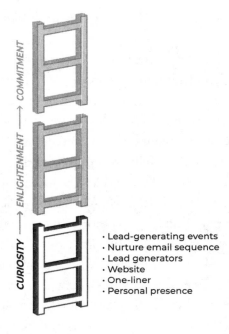

- Lead-generating events
- Nurture email sequence
- Lead generators
- Website
- One-liner
- Personal presence

WHAT IS IT LIKE FOR A CLIENT TO MEET YOU?

Imagine what it is like to meet you in person. Be honest. What is it like to encounter you at a cocktail party or spend an hour with you having lunch? If *you* were meeting *you* for the first time, would you bet your career on your coaching? After all, that is what you are asking all your clients to do. You are asking your clients to bet their livelihood on the wisdom you carry and the community you curate.

Take an honest, thoughtful look at yourself. Are you calm? Are you a good listener? When meeting with you, does it feel as though you are rushing through a sales pitch? How are you dressed? Do you come off as competent? Are you too self-deprecating to take seriously? Or, are you the opposite: arrogant and condescending, a sure sign of insecurity?

You are the largest billboard for your business. Your calm demeanor, ability to see the world from your client's point of view, ability to empathize and even communicate your empathy, and yes, even the way you are dressed (as though you take yourself and your job and your clients seriously) will either pique a client's curiosity or turn them off.

The goal for you is this: You want your clients to feel you have something they need. And that something is a peaceful, organized mind when it comes to building a business.

If you follow the steps in this book, you will not have to fake this peaceful confidence. You will truly have your stuff together and your very presence will show that you care and that you know what you are doing.

Once your presence is centered, you will then want a way to express an honest offer. This is where your **one-liner** comes in. (Basically an elevator pitch.) If you've yet to create your one-liner then do so now because it will be a critical aid in successful networking.

After communicating your practiced and polished one-liner, you have some choices. If you feel the client is interested to know more, send them on to one of the pieces of marketing collateral you've created to enlighten potential clients about how your coaching can help them. If you think the client's curiosity is piqued but they don't seem motivated to start their journey, send them to another curiosity tool, such as your landing page, a lead generator, or a live event. Perhaps your client should come to the monthly breakfast you curate or attend a webinar. Regardless, when you know what your curiosity tools are, you will know what to do with unpaying, potential clients: Direct them to your curiosity material.

What curiosity tools can you use to pique your clients' curiosity and help them enter into the enlightenment phase of their relationship with you as a coach?

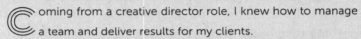

COACH'S STORY

Coming from a creative director role, I knew how to manage a team and deliver results for my clients.

But my young family needed more of me than was left over after the grueling hours.

What I didn't know how to do was build my business or "be a coach."

I struggled at first—trying to act like other coaches and convince potential clients to trust me.

Yes, I had the frameworks and knew people would get results . . . but, why would anybody pay *me*?

Then, through a community of coaches, I realized clients were drawn to me for the energy and clarity I brought (the exact things I'd tried to stifle as a coach).

As I started showing up as myself, more people were drawn in, more contracts were signed, and my confidence grew.

Fast-forward a couple years. I'm making more money than ever before, working half the hours, and I'm present daily in my kids' lives.

The kicker was last month. Someone asked my daughter what I do for work. She quickly replied, "My daddy smiles all day long and helps people like their businesses again. And that's what I want to do when I grow up."

—JAKE BROWN,
business coach since 2021

How Can You Pique Your Clients' Curiosity?

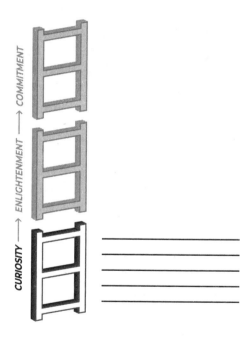

Examples of curiosity tools include: your one-liner, your business card (with your one-liner printed on the back), your website, your lead generators, your in-person events such as small business breakfasts, coffees, inspirational speaker events, your own presentations, and so on. Fill out the blank lines on the previous page. Start with a single curiosity step and expand from there. I recommend that you have at least three curiosity steps designed specifically to pique your clients' curiosity about how you can help them survive and thrive.

Once you've added a few curiosity steps to your client journey, they will likely move into the enlightenment phase.

It's true that some of your curiosity tools will overlap into enlightenment territory, but that is fine. The line between curiosity and enlightenment is a bit blurry, but you understand the general idea: Clients move from short sound bites into longer explanations, all of which get satisfied by the marketing collateral you create.

PHASE TWO: ENLIGHTENMENT

Once a client's curiosity is piqued, you will want to enlighten them about how your coaching service will benefit them specifically. The main question any potential client is going to have is this: *Will this work for me?* Your enlightenment collateral will then answer that question and more.

If a future client has gone to your website, downloaded your lead generator, taken an assessment, or scheduled an hour of your time, they are more than curious. They are now wondering whether or not to invest in your coaching.

When a client engages a piece of marketing collateral or an entry-level product, it means they want to get to know you. This is an important phase in any long-term relationship and it can't be skipped. Essentially, your client has started "dating" you and they are, especially in these early phases, assessing the worth of your coaching.

If it helps, you can think of it this way: The enlightenment collateral you create will give potential clients a free (or inexpensive) taste of your products and services.

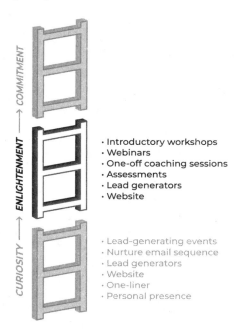

- Introductory workshops
- Webinars
- One-off coaching sessions
- Assessments
- Lead generators
- Website

- Lead-generating events
- Nurture email sequence
- Lead generators
- Website
- One-liner
- Personal presence

Giving the client baby steps they can take into the enlightenment phase honors the emotional journey involved in making a big decision, such as investing in coaching. I learned how important this was when, years ago, I invited about forty business leaders to Nashville for a one-day mastermind. The mastermind session was a reward for having purchased at least fifty copies of my newest book. I never intended for the interaction to move beyond that, but I enjoyed the mastermind so much I decided to turn around and invite all of the attendees to a biannual in-person meeting combined with a monthly group Zoom call. I charged a healthy fee for the new mastermind and was pleased to discover more than 40 percent of the original attendees decided to engage the offer. I do not believe more than 10 percent would have engaged the offer without the introductory, risk-free event. That's the power of creating marketing and introductory product collateral to cover the enlightenment phase of the client journey.

Why was the introductory event so important in the sales sequence? Because it gave people a test drive of the product and enlightened them about the value they would receive.

How Can You Enlighten Your Clients About the Value They Will Receive?

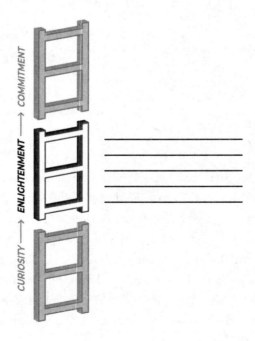

Examples of enlightenment tools include: your website, your lead generators, your keynote presentations, your assessments, your one-off, topic-driven coaching sessions, your one-day introductory workshops, your webinars, and so on.

PHASE THREE: COMMITMENT

Some clients will move through the curiosity and enlightenment phases quickly, and some will take years. This hardly matters to you, though. What matters is that you've created enough collateral in all three phases so as to move your clients through at their own pace. They will take the next step whenever they feel safe and comfortable doing so. Your job, then, is to make sure their next step exists and that they know about it when they feel the need to move forward.

The final phase, of course, is the commitment phase. When a client enters into the commitment phase it means they are willing to invest their money, their time, and their future by engaging you as a coach.

That said, there is still a hierarchy of investment willingness. Some clients will only want to attend your basic-level mastermind and others may want one-on-one coaching, workshops, or to join an elite-level mastermind.

As a general rule, about 10 percent of your paying clients will pay you ten times more for something else as long as you have packaged enough value for them and made the offer clear. Here's what I mean by that: If you have one thousand clients paying you $100 for an entry-level product (likely digital), you can safely count on about one hundred of those clients being willing to pay you $1,000 for a stronger engagement, whether that is a large, one-day conference, or something like an elite-level digital product.

Of those one hundred clients willing to pay you $1,000, there will be about ten who are willing to pay you $10,000 for even more engagement, such as an elite-level mastermind or a private workshop in which you lead their team through a valuable learning experience, such as leadership, sales, or marketing training.

The great news for you as a coach is that if you create a hierarchy of products, a percentage of your existing customers who get value from your coaching will invest in more and more. This means your business grows without having to constantly find new clients. There is plenty of growth opportunity for you in your existing clientele.

This truth became known to me when I spent a day with a friend who was also a fan of my coaching. He was such a fan that he had actually introduced some of my frameworks to dozens of his friends, each of whom had invested $275 in one of my digital products. In a candid conversation, my friend told me that he called each of his friends and asked how they felt about my brand and my offering. Each of them gave the same response, my friend said. They said this: *I love Don's work; my only complaint is I feel guilty. He has made me a lot of money but I don't have a way of paying him back. If he had a higher-level product, I would buy it.*

After that conversation, I got to work on my own menu of products and created higher-tier products so more of my existing clients could further engage my coaching services. You can learn from me and create your own hierarchy of products much sooner.

Make sure your products start as low-priced entry products and extend up as high as you believe clients will be willing to go. As long as you provide more and more value, a percentage of your clients will pay that price to receive more and more of your coaching.

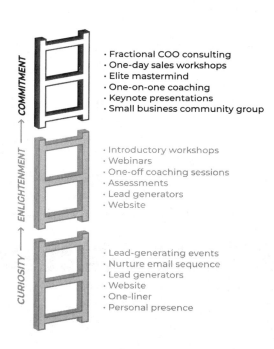

- Fractional COO consulting
- One-day sales workshops
- Elite mastermind
- One-on-one coaching
- Keynote presentations
- Small business community group

- Introductory workshops
- Webinars
- One-off coaching sessions
- Assessments
- Lead generators
- Website

- Lead-generating events
- Nurture email sequence
- Lead generators
- Website
- One-liner
- Personal presence

What Is Your Hierarchy of Products?

Examples of commitment products include: your entry-level community group, your elite masterminds, your one-on-one coaching, your private sales, leadership, or marketing workshops, your private, demographic-oriented elite-level masterminds, and your fractional COO, CRO, or CMO services.

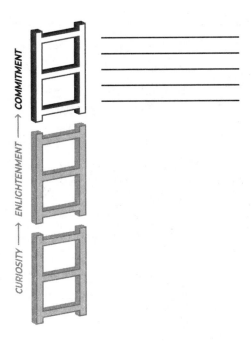

COACH'S STORY

t was 2021 and I was working a W2 job as an executive coach and organizational development consultant for a large healthcare system. I had been coaching for ten years, but always "inside" of organizations. W2s are safe and provide healthcare benefits and 401(k) match. On paper, it's the safe bet. I liked safe. But I wasn't willing to accept having a ceiling on my salary and a stranglehold on my calendar/availability.

When I joined a coaching community I was already earning a side income as a speaker, coach, and leadership development facilitator. I needed a certain level of confidence that I could actually make ends meet before taking the leap into full-time solopreneur. (It's almost humorous typing this now, three years later . . .)

In January of 2021, one of my previous clients reached out and asked me to speak at his company's annual sales kickoff. This was a well-known tech company and promised to be a great event for personal exposure. Armed with my knowledge of several coaching frameworks, I turned a solid $4,000 speaking opportunity into a golden chance to "sell from the stage."

How did I do this? I met with the client to understand the pain points of the listeners and dialed in the content to be A+. This is a tedious, but worthwhile process. Had I been doing this talk before knowing how to be a better coach, I would have stopped here.

Instead, here's what I did:

1. I asked the sponsor if I could offer additional coaching to those who were interested. (I learned from my relationship with the sponsor that each employee had $2,000 per year of professional development to use however they wished.)

2. I created a four-week group coaching program that went deeper into the topic I covered onstage (How to Communicate to Drive Results), teaching them a framework they could use in their selling situations with prospects and customers.

3. I wireframed a simple sales/landing page using the StoryBrand seven-part framework.

4.   I placed a colorful call-to-action button on the landing page (SIGN UP NOW) that took payment right away.

As I finished my seventy-five-minute talk, I briefly covered the information about signing up for the group coaching cohort and then said goodbye to the five-hundred-plus participants on the video call.

Relieved that the energy was great and the talk went well, I sat down at my desk and took a breath . . .

. . . and then the crazy thing happened. My email starting dinging. And dinging. Each new alert in my inbox was someone registering for the group coaching cohort. In a matter of thirty minutes, two cohorts were completely filled and the wait list was growing.

Once the dust settled, I realized that my $4,000 speaking gig turned into a $50,000 revenue capture (by being ready to move people into the group coaching sessions). I was able to continue to serve those clients in different ways over the next year, which yielded an additional $10,000 in revenue from workshops that I conducted.

I was well on my way to replacing my W2 income. With one speaking event, I had accounted for a third of my typical salary. I was on to something and had a recipe for success.

Without the confidence those frameworks gave me, I wouldn't have even considered selling from the stage and having an offer ready to go for those participants who wanted to go deeper into a coaching relationship with me. In other words, I would not have capitalized on the expertise I possessed that others needed and wanted.

It's been almost three years since that event, and I'm well on my way to having the best revenue year of my career to date . . . all as a solo coach/speaker/facilitator.

—JASON DAILY,
business coach since 2011

CREATE YOUR CLIENT LADDER
AND LET THE LADDER DO THE WORK

If all of this sounds intimidating, don't worry. Every piece of marketing collateral or product offering you create will help you grow your coaching business. You don't have to create it all at once.

All you need to do now is create a ladder and then slowly create each piece of collateral on the ladder. For some, this will take months and for others, years. Many coaches will find that their schedule fills up well before they finish creating all the marketing and product collateral they intended to create. If this happens to you, congratulations. That said, completing each piece of marketing and product collateral will help you scale your coaching business into a coaching agency, if that's something you desire. I will talk more about that in a later chapter.

For now, though, just know that mapping your client journey will give you extreme clarity about what you offer, where each of your clients is on the journey you're inviting them into, and how your coaching business is going to grow.

Once you have your list of products created, your marketing plan in place, and your customer journey mapped, it's time to set some goals about how quickly, and how big, you want your coaching business to grow.

Let's talk about goal-setting, specifically for coaches, in the next chapter.

STEP SIX

Establish Realistic Goals and Accomplish Those Goals

Now that we've worked through the fundamental blocks of building a coaching business, let's establish some goals that will put flesh on the vision and keep us motivated. Most of us have the goal of starting a coaching business, but few of us have broken down our goals into specific categories that will keep us motivated and on track.

Without goals, you're on a road to nowhere. As a coach, you already know that. But a startling number of coaches I meet have absolutely no business goals themselves, even while assigning goal-setting exercises to their clients. This is total hypocrisy. We've got to live out our coaching advice in our own businesses if we expect to succeed ourselves.

If we want to build a successful coaching business that will impact the most clients and allow us to build personal wealth in the process, I recommend setting goals in three critical areas. The three critical areas are Revenue, Qualified Leads, and Products Sold.

Revenue. You will be much more motivated to grow your coaching business if it pays well. So, how much money do you want to make as a small business coach? $85,000? $125,000? $250,000?

The best way to establish your revenue goal is to ask yourself how much money you will need to live on, how much money you'd like to invest, and how much money you'd like to use for generosity. Add those numbers together and you've got a financial number you can head toward.

Once you break down your revenue goals into three categories (your lifestyle, your investments, and your generosity), the number may be slightly more than you previously thought. That's okay. The larger the number, the more ambitious your goal. Feel free to dream big. In the end, business is all about trading dollars for solutions, and if you've taken the steps in this book you will have plenty of solutions clients will be happy to pay for.

Reaching your overall salary goal may take one or two years, but if you work the steps in this book, and if you are a good coach, you will get there.

Qualified Leads. In order to reach your revenue goal, you are going to need to set a goal for qualified leads. Without leads, you will have nobody to convert into paying clients and no way to build revenue. It goes without saying that the larger your revenue goal, the more leads you are going to need to hit those goals.

If you would like to coach twenty clients per month either one-on-one or in a small group, you will likely need about eighteen new leads per month to achieve that goal within the first year. Why? Because approximately 10 percent of the relationships you build (either in person or through your automated email campaigns) will become paying clients.

If you introduce your services to 216 qualified leads within a calendar year (at eighteen per month), for instance, you will find that 21.6 of those will become paying clients. For this reason, you want to establish the goal of collecting a set number of new qualified leads each month. To reach your goal of twenty paying clients, you will need eighteen qualified leads per month. If you want thirty paying clients, you will need twenty-five new leads each month. Attracting this many leads may not sound too difficult, but it will definitely require a focused effort.

Products Sold. Of course your revenue and salary will only grow if you are able to sell products. Once you establish a way (or several ways) of acquiring leads, you will want to convert those leads into paying customers. The best way to do this is to identify the problem your clients are struggling with and then offer a coaching product that solves their problem.

Setting a revenue goal by itself is a great start, but you aren't likely to hit that goal unless you know *how* you are going to hit that goal. And how are you going to hit that goal? You will hit your revenue goal by selling a certain number of each of your coaching products.

That's why your lead and revenue goals should be broken down per piece of marketing collateral and per product. Essentially, you want to establish a goal for every item on your client ladder. Your goal lists (based on twelve weeks) might look like this:

MARKETING GOALS		
One-liner exposure and business card	10 per week	120 total
Website visits	250 per week	3,000 total

MARKETING GOALS		
Lead generator 1 download—PDF	40 per week	480 total
Lead generator 2 downloads—online assessment	40 per week	480 total
Sales email captured and processed	20 per week	240 total

PRODUCT SOLD GOALS		
Introductory assessment coaching call	24 clients	$199 per
Introductory topic-driven coaching call	12 clients	$199 per
New additions to my Small Business Community Group	24 clients	$249 per
Monthly elite mastermind	12 clients	$800 per client per month
Sales training workshop	4 clients	$10,000 per
Leadership strategy workshop	4 clients	$10,000 per
One-on-one bimonthly coaching	6 clients	$800 per client per month
Fractional COO service	2 clients	$25,000 per

If the coach who set these specific goals reaches their annual goal per product, their run rate by the end of the year will involve, approximately, $4,766 for their introductory coaching assessment calls, $2,388 for their introductory topic-driven coaching calls, $5,976 for their small business community group, $115,200 for their monthly elite mastermind, $40,000 for their sales training workshops, $40,000 for their leadership strategy workshops, $57,600 for their one-on-one coaching sessions, and $50,000 for their fractional COO services.

This is an example of a terrifically successful coach who is without question very busy, but we can dream, can't we? This coach's annual revenue would be $315,930.

As long as this coach establishes goals for their lead measures, those being marketing funnel goals, they should be able to reach their product sales goals, too.

It might take twenty-four to thirty-six months for a new coach to build their client list up to this level but it is certainly doable if they earn the reputation of a coach who delivers results. I have known many coaches who pivot their career and make even more money than this in as little as six months.

Of course, you can set more goals than the three categories I've included here, but I'd consider these three categories foundational and necessary.

TO GROW YOUR BUSINESS, HIT YOUR GOALS

Goals are great, but unless they are taken seriously, they aren't helpful. In order to hit our goals we will need to make sacrifices, mainly in the area of our time. Several hours each morning that are set aside for building our coaching businesses will be required. Goals aren't magical; they're just a point on a map. To get there, we have to start walking, and if our goals are ambitious, we have to keep walking when everybody else has quit.

TO HIT YOUR GOALS, TAKE ACTION

As a coach, you've likely noticed how diverse really successful people are. Some are intelligent; some aren't so bright. Some are loud;

some are quiet. Some are charming; others are dull. In fact, it would be easy to think there's no specific kind of person who succeeds. Except. Except for one characteristic they all have: Successful people have a strong bias toward action. They move. They do things. They make things exist that previously didn't exist.

You've likely noticed this in your clients. You can coach one client for years and they just can't seem to get it done, and yet another, with only a spoonful of knowledge, will move mountains. The difference is in their willingness to take action, of course. If this is true for our clients, it's true for us, too.

The power of doing things being even more effective than getting lost in thought was a paradigm shift for me. I experienced the shift, in part, while listening to an audiobook called *Relentless* by Tim Grover. Grover trained Michael Jordan during and through his prime. What intrigued me while listening to the book was the differentiator Grover said set the world's most elite athletes apart. It was not skill or intelligence, though many of the world's elite athletes have both. It was, rather, the relentless drive to win met with the willingness to take action.

The point is this: While so many people are strategizing to succeed, those who do succeed at the highest level are the ones who get out of bed and make it happen.

If you bought this book, you might be the kind of person who likes to prepare. But you also might be the kind of person who gets stuck preparing and never makes a move.

Make a move.

Before you do, though, here's what's going to happen the second you start building or growing your coaching business: You are going to feel lost. You are going to feel like you don't know what you're doing. You are going to want to stop doing and start thinking again.

Don't misunderstand me. Preparation is important. When we prepare, our actions go further and have a larger impact. But you will never, ever be 100 percent ready. At some point, we have to move toward our goals with a dogged determination that plows through distraction.

Can you imagine if Michael Jordan or Usain Bolt or Serena Williams or any other world-class athlete decided not to play until they were completely ready? If they waited until they felt ready, we wouldn't even know who they are. No. World-class athletes, and for that matter world-class coaches, play injured. They play afraid. They play in the face of pressure. They move and they move because they've all discovered moving is their secret advantage. Let everybody else think it over one more time. While the competition is thinking, you will be running toward the finish line.

No matter how good your plan is, it's going to feel incomplete. Work it anyway. You can fix things while you are moving. Make no excuses. Hit those goals.

WHAT TO DO IF YOU FAIL

Business coaches are ambitious people. They have to be. How else are we going to help our clients win? But for a person who psychologically sinks or swims based on whether or not they achieve their goals, falling short can be debilitating.

Being totally destroyed because you didn't hit your goals is a good thing, though. If it bothers you to not hit your goals, it means you don't like to settle for anything less than excellence, which is a good thing for anybody who eventually wants to win.

When you fail to reach your goals, take some advice from, well, yourself. I mean that. What would you say to a client who did well but failed to reach their ambitious goals? Of course you'd counsel them to look at all they got right, duplicate those efforts, then list all they got wrong and learn from those mistakes.

There have been plenty of years when I did not reach my business goals but, looking back, those have been the years that fostered the greatest creativity and dedication. In fact, I often tell my clients, "You are only a few big mistakes away from being a master at your craft."

Another thing to think about when you fail to reach your goals is whether or not your goals were actually too ambitious for this stage of your coaching business. If you're looking to build a multimillion-dollar coaching business, it will take time to organize your offering, clarify your message, grow your client list, hire coaches to work under you, and learn how to operate such a business. Let's not expect extreme success overnight.

REVIEW YOUR GOALS WEEKLY AND ADJUST YOUR STRATEGY AS YOU GO

You will want to review your goals, along with where you are measuring up against those goals, often. In fact, it's not a bad idea to review your goals as part of your morning ritual. If you have a team, consider reviewing your agency goals once each week during your All-Staff Meeting.

When you review your goals, you will know whether or not you are behind on attracting qualified leads and adjust by creating a new lead generator or perhaps promoting an existing lead generator. Looking at your revenue goals will tell you whether or not you need to add a new paying client or perhaps raise your prices. We will only adjust our strategy (and motivation) when our goals remain ever-present in our minds.

Lastly, when you hit your goals, celebrate. If it's a small goal, treat yourself to a nice cigar or a day at the spa. If you reach a large goal, buy yourself a watch or a big date night with your spouse. If you have a team, take them all to a movie if you hit a small goal or take them on a trip if you hit a big goal.

The reason you want to celebrate your goals is because it will increase your momentum and prevent burnout. If you are only grinding in order to keep grinding, you will not enjoy your business, but if your business offers you hard, meaningful work followed by pleasurable rewards, the virtuous cycle will generate terrific results and an even better quality of life.

My hope is the first six steps in this book will ensure you succeed as a business coach. Let's talk now about sharing your achievements (and challenges) with a community.

When you're a coach, you are constantly pouring out your heart and mind for the benefit of others. Unless you have a community pouring back into you, you're likely to burn out. The next step in growing your coaching business, then, is not so much about growing your business as it is about growing yourself.

Next, let's talk about the power of surrounding yourself with a community of coaches you call friends.

STEP SEVEN

Build or Join a Coaching Community That Will Help You Grow Yourself and Your Business

very other week I meet with my business coach. My coach has helped me address leadership challenges, set revenue goals, vision cast for myself and my family, and much more. Why do I meet with a business coach? Because I believe in the power of coaching, not just for my clients but for myself.

Not only this, but every month I meet with a group of coaches to share best practices and encouragement. We meet on a Zoom call on a set day each month and talk about the challenges we've encountered in the previous month. I've yet to be on one of those calls in which I didn't gain valuable insight, not to mention encouragement and support.

Every great coach can tell a story about somebody who coached them, and many of them can also tell stories about the community of coaches they interact with on a weekly or monthly basis. Good coaches hang around other good coaches.

One of my favorite documentaries is called *The Art of Coaching*, which captures an annual get-together between college football coach Nick Saban and professional football coach Bill Belichick. Combined, the two coaches have won thirteen national championships or Super Bowls. Decades ago, the two coaches worked together in Cleveland and have remained friends ever since.

Watching the two men talk, it became obvious to me why they've both succeeded. They are each intensely curious about the answer to two questions: In football, what works and what doesn't? That's really it. In fact, they are more than curious; they are obsessed with the answer to these two questions. Neither Coach Saban nor Coach Belichick is satisfied with their current level of football understanding. Instead, they continue looking for new ways to win.

Early in the documentary, Coach Belichick asked the crew to leave the room. He and Coach Saban hadn't seen each other in nearly a year and so Coach Belichick wanted to catch up, personally, before they started filming. The crew left the room but accidentally left the cameras and microphones rolling and I was somewhat humored by what happened next. Coach Belichick watched as the crew left, greeted Coach Saban with a personal gesture, and sat down. I thought Coach Belichick might ask a personal question about Coach Saban's family or his health, but he didn't. Instead, Coach Belichick's first question was about the kind of defense Saban had run the previous year at Alabama. In other words, these two men are so obsessed with winning in football that even their private, personal conversations are about football. I couldn't help but laugh at the exchange. And yet it's telling, isn't it? Find me somebody who succeeds at the highest level and I'll show you somebody who is affected by an obsession.

My point in telling the story of Belichick and Saban isn't about obsession, though; it's about friendship and community. There are only a handful of people in the entire world these two men can talk to about their obsession. Most football coaches want to win, but are most football coaches obsessed?

What is it that generates greatness in a human being? I'd put money on three things: an obsession with what works, an ability to distill what works into repeatable processes, and, finally, the community that helps them develop and execute on what works.

Most business coaches—in fact, most entrepreneurs—have the first two items on that list deeply embedded in their DNA. It's the third element that many of us struggle with. We just don't get together with other coaches and exchange information we can use to improve our results and our clients' results.

MEETING WITH OTHER COACHES WILL HELP YOU GENERATE BETTER RESULTS FOR YOUR CLIENTS

We business coaches can learn a thing or two from psychiatrists and therapists, not just personally, but professionally. I have a few friends who run successful counseling practices and was interested to discover that many counseling practices hold regular meetings in which their therapists talk to each other about their clients' challenges. I'm not talking about gossip. I'm talking about a routine meeting in which the therapists share what's going on in their clients' worlds and the other therapists speak into the treatment the therapist is offering. The result? The clients themselves get the wisdom of multiple counselors speaking into their lives. Of course, these conversations are confidential and the clients themselves (who are not in the meeting with the other therapists) agree to the process, but who wouldn't? If there are four therapists in the private meeting, the client is getting four times the perspective and wisdom.

As much as a clear website, lead generator, and an email nurturing system will build your business, meeting with other coaches may actually be more important, because those other coaches will have wisdom about creating a clear website, lead generators, email campaigns, and all the rest of the foundational business practices. Add to that the emotional encouragement we get when we involve ourselves in a coaching community and you'll discover community is a critical element in the growth of your coaching business.

MEETING WITH OTHER COACHES CAN HELP YOU GROW YOUR OWN BUSINESS

Another meeting I attend once each year is a meeting with about ten other business writers. We usually get together at my house and spend a day discussing how to build a better writing and speaking business. Because of these meetings, my books are better written because I've learned a great deal more about how to structure a book, my books sell better because I've learned a great deal more about how to sell a book, my speaking honorariums have gone up because I've learned what my actual value is, and on top of that, I have learned more about how to structure a talk for maximum impact.

I'd say the knowledge I get during that annual, one-day writers meeting is more than I've received in the fifty or more books I've read about writing and speaking. There are few experiences more powerful than getting together with a group of accomplished peers with the focused intent of discovering how we can get better at our craft.

I believe so much in the power of these meetings that every year in Nashville my company, Business Made Simple, hosts a summit in which our certified business coaches and our certified marketing professionals get together to share best practices.

At the summit, we bring in speakers and entertainment, but I'm quite honest with the community that there's nothing we can provide that will grow their individual businesses faster than the informal conversations they will have around their lunch and dinner tables. It's the honest exchanges about what's working and what's not working that improve our abilities the most.

WITHOUT COMMUNITY WE CAN SCREW UP OUR CAREERS AND OUR LIVES

Every once in a while you see a leader implode. It can be painful to watch. When a business, religious, or political leader implodes it's usually the last step in a long journey that was headed toward an implosion from the beginning.

The first step to an implosion, in my view, is some form of conscious or subconscious elitism. The leader was part of a community and in that community the leader shared best practices with their peers as an equal. As the leader became a little more successful than their peers, though, they began to give more advice than they received.

This tendency to think of ourselves as superior to others isn't generated from a place of strength, by the way. It's generated from a wound.

The reason the leader wanted to succeed in the first place may have been because they wanted to prove all their detractors wrong. They believed they were special and were out to prove it. Once they proved it, and once everybody agreed they were talented, their ego became less and less comfortable receiving advice from their peers. If anybody dared speak truth into the person's life, they backed out of that relationship and slowly began replacing their sources of honest feedback with minions who fed their ego. Separated, then, from the truth about their own character flaws, they began to believe the voices within their own echo chamber and bought into the idea that they were special, that the rules didn't apply to them. And that's when they started breaking the rules. After which they got caught. After which they imploded and their career was destroyed.

Nearly every prominent leader who has imploded has followed this exact path. Some of these leaders have been able to rebuild, but most leaders who suffer this kind of implosion are unable to regain the influence they once enjoyed.

How did the fall of the leader start? It started when they stopped listening to their community and replaced that community with an elevated image of self. It started when they no longer believed the truth that we all have challenges that need to be addressed and that those challenges never end.

The truth about success is it comes from hard work, humility, and resilience. Often, people who succeed get a little cocky when they get to the top and mistakenly believe it's the cockiness that shaped them. I assure you, cockiness doesn't matter. What got them there was the work, the devotion, and the community of great players and coaches and trainers they spent time with.

Not long ago, I watched an interview with Warren Buffett. The interviewer asked Buffett about the secret to his success, and instead of answering the question, Buffett began talking about his terrific assistant, his lifelong business partners, and his incredible team. He talked about his home life, how he's only gotten on two flights in the last two years because he likes being home with his family and friends. At one point in the interview, Buffett even explained that, at ninety-two years old, he wasn't even the senior source of wisdom in his firm, that his partner Charlie Munger, who was ninety-nine at the time, was a critical factor in his own success. Buffett explained he only had a normal level of intelligence, that there was nothing special about him, and that his success was built on a genuine curiosity about what makes a business successful and, above all else, friendships with those who also love the game of investing.

All forms of coaching, including business coaching, can cause serious distortions in your ego. The more advice you give, and the better results your clients experience, the more tempting it will be to believe there is something special about you. Don't fall for it. In fact, if you want to be the greatest ever, commit to letting other people believe you are the greatest but never believe it about yourself. Stay humble. Keep learning. Stay in community.

Most leaders who fall from their elevated positions have one thing in common: They were alone when they fell. They'd already pushed everybody else away.

IF YOU DON'T HAVE A COMMUNITY, BUILD ONE

So what do you do if you don't have a community of coaches you can share time with? You create one.

If you've never created a community, don't overthink it. Honestly, community is created very simply. A community tends to take shape when the same people get together several times. That's really it. It may seem awkward to bring a group of coaches together to talk about your coaching businesses, but you will find the awkwardness goes away the more times you meet.

The problem is, most people who try to create a community never get past the second or third awkward meeting. They just think that the group isn't working and people aren't opening up or sharing anything of value. Don't let that stop you from meeting. Keep going. Community takes time, but once it's created, the benefits are substantial.

What you will find, over time, is that after the tenth or twelfth meeting, you begin to connect as old friends working together on the same team. For years, I met every six weeks with a group of Black-owned-business owners. For the first five or six meetings, I definitely felt like the only white guy, not quite sure how I fit into the group I'd started. These days, that group feels like family. Our little cohort went from stiff, uncomfortable meetings in which a group of strangers discussed our goals to friends that became deeply invested in each other's stories. And what was the recipe for this success? It was time. It wasn't the format we created or the questions we asked or the frameworks we discussed. It was just the power of time spent.

THE GREAT ONES HANG TOGETHER

People who achieve cultural and intellectual significance don't just become great because they work hard, although they certainly work hard. They become great because they spur each other on to become great. Did you know, for instance, that Leonardo DiCaprio and Tobey Maguire were good friends long before either of them became famous? So were Matt Damon and Ben Affleck.

I wasn't surprised to read a few years ago that my favorite psychologist, Viktor Frankl, had befriended Sigmund Freud when Frankl was only a teen in Vienna. Carl Jung also famously came to Vienna for a thirteen-hour meeting with Freud. Have you ever wondered why Vienna produced so many foundational psychologists between 1880 and 1950? Alfred Adler, Sigmund Freud, Viktor Frankl, Josef Breuer, Anna Freud, Melanie Klein, and a few years later, Heinz Kohut and Bruno Bettelheim. Each of these psychologists came out of Vienna around the turn of the twentieth century. Coincidence? I doubt it. I think it's more likely that humans are communal beings, and the better their communities, the more impactful their work.

At the turn of the twentieth century, Vienna had a robust university system combined with a coffee-shop culture that fostered open collaboration. Were psychologists in Austria and Switzerland more intelligent than psychologists in America, Japan, or Zimbabwe? It's doubtful. They just talked to each other a great deal more, which is why and how they created such foundational works. Not only this, they published in the same journals, lectured in the same lecture halls, and built upon each other's work.

The same can be said about classical music in Vienna and ballet in Russia, acting in Hollywood, auto manufacturing in Detroit, hockey in Canada, and on and on and on.

Our communities are greater predictors of our success than most of us are aware of. Thomas Jefferson and John Adams were famously connected as both friends and rivals, writing letters to each other until their deaths on the same day: July 4, 1826. Their friendship spurred each other to create foundational works on which democratic ideas are still built today. Toward the end of their lives, Adams wrote to Jefferson:

> A letter from you calls up recollections very dear to my mind. It carries me back to the times when, beset with difficulties and dangers, we are fellow laborers in the same cause, struggling for what is most valuable to man, his right of self-government. Laboring always at the same oar, with some wave ever ahead threatening to overwhelm us and yet passing harmless under our bark, we knew not how, we rode through the storm with heart and hand, and made a happy port.

Here is the truth: If you play on a team that is advancing a great cause, you will go much further in your life and career than you will working alone.

We are not independent creatures. We are designed to join a community and strengthen each other to better serve the world.

There are plenty of other business coaches in your area. There's likely another business coach in your own neighborhood. Ask around. Post something on your social media channels that says you're looking for other coaches. Get together for coffee, and keep getting together until you become friends. Spur each other on. It's harder to quit when you're doing something hard with friends.

If you don't have a community of coaches, find one or create one. Your success and the success of your clients may depend upon the community you join or create.

STEP EIGHT

Master the Soft Skills
of Coaching

So far we've talked mostly about the playbooks, processes, and frameworks required to build a successful coaching business. But as we all know, much of your success will depend on soft skills. In short, to be a good coach we need to be good with people and, well, people are complicated.

When we talk about soft skills, we are really talking about the characteristics it takes for a coach to build trust with their clients.

As much as I believe in playbooks and frameworks, if you're bad with people, your coaching business will fail.

In a way, this chapter feels unnecessary in a book for those who want to be coaches. Anybody interested in coaching is likely already great with people. One of the reasons this book focuses so much on a step-by-step playbook is because you likely already have the people stuff figured out.

And yet, sharpening the skills necessary to connect can only help. So the chapter stays in the book. The better we are with people, the better "product" we will deliver as a coach. After all, coaching is, above all, a relationship with a client.

To start, though, let's discuss a paradigm shift that many coaches who have gone before us have figured out over the years: You are not going to be close friends with your clients. Don't get me wrong—in many ways, the kind of relationship you will have with your clients will be even closer than that of a friendship. The reality is, however, most coaching clients aren't looking for a friend. What they're looking for (perhaps without even knowing so) is a mentor, somebody who knows more than they do and can teach them what to do with the challenging situation they are in.

With that, let's look at some soft skills that will help us deliver incredible coaching. Here are five characteristics great coaches have in common when it comes to building a trusting relationship.

CHARACTERISTIC ONE: THEY PLAY THE GUIDE

The sooner a coach accepts their responsibility as a guide in their clients' lives, the more their clients will actually get out of the relationship.

What is a guide? A guide is the character in the story that exists purely to help the hero win.

The guide is important in a story because, without the guide, the hero would be lost. The guide, then, steps into the story and helps the hero know what to do, usually based on the guide's backstory in which they conquered the very challenge threatening the hero today.

While the story is always about the hero, the hero is not the strongest character in the narrative. The guide, in fact, is the strongest character. The guide has overcome the hero's fear, developed a plan, trained other heroes, and gives emotional support (and practical wisdom) the hero can use to win the day.

What are the characteristics of a guide? There are many, but here are the two that are the most important:

1. **They are empathetic:** When we identify, understand, and are able to share in our clients' frustrations, we create a bond with them that goes deep. As small business owners, our clients often feel overwhelmed and even trapped; otherwise, they likely wouldn't have sought out our coaching. Statements such as "I remember when this happened in my own business. I was just as frustrated as you are right now . . ." go far to alleviate a sense of aloneness our clients might feel. As it relates to empathy with our clients, the overwhelming perspective we must have is this: Your pain is my pain.

2. **They are competent:** As coaches, of course, we have to do more than just share in our clients' pain; we have to help them find relief from that pain. After empathizing with our clients' frustrations, we must be equipped to give them a plan that will resolve their frustrations and help them execute that plan.

As you help your clients resolve their problems, make sure to remember that, from you, they are looking for an empathetic authority figure who is both understanding and capable of helping them solve their problems.

CHARACTERISTIC TWO:
THEY DON'T RUSH THE PROCESS

One of the hardest coaching qualities to develop is patience. Because you already know what the client should do and how they should do it, you're going to expect them to arrive at your next session having taken a giant leap forward only to discover they've hardly moved an inch. Wow. How can they possibly not have done their homework?

The main reason they are moving so slowly is because they are just beginning to understand the concepts you have been familiar with for years. As it relates to the information and assignments you are giving them, everything is new, and that's okay. What may look like inches of progress to you could feel like miles to them. If you are patient with your clients, they will get to the results soon enough, but if you rush the process, they will likely grow weary and quit.

Along with being patient with our clients, we want to be persistent. Patience and persistence are not mutually exclusive characteristics. Though our client must move at their own pace, they must move forward or they will not benefit from our coaching. If it takes your client a month to write their mission statement, so be it. Let's just make sure their mission statement actually gets written. While it's okay to move slow, as coaches it is still our job to help our client produce results.

CHARACTERISTIC THREE: THEY LEAD THEIR CLIENTS ON A JOURNEY OF SELF DISCOVERY

We've all been there. We are able to see exactly what a client should do in order to experience a breakthrough, but the more we press, the less they move. Why? There are many reasons, including the fact that nobody likes to be pushed or controlled. The truth is, we can't realize an idea for a client; they have to realize it themselves. What we can do, though, is share principles.

For instance, it is a principle that a small business should be focused on a series of economic objectives. This principle may seem obvious to you and me but it won't be obvious to your client. In fact, in order to define their economic objectives and include them in their mission, they will need to realize the following:

1. If they don't start focusing on making money, their business is going to go under.

2. They earn most of their profitable dollars off only a few of their products.

3. If they talk openly about how the business makes money, their staff will start seeing the business as a business rather than an early retirement arrangement.

In addition to these ideas, the client needs to start "realizing" that specific products don't make them the kind of money they thought they did and begin asking if certain products shouldn't be dropped in favor of more profitable products.

They need to realize that they should not bear the revenue burden alone. They need to realize that they should be getting revenue projection reports. They need to realize that their administrative costs are too high. They need to realize a lot of stuff that, to you, is as plain as the nose on their face, a nose, by the way, that they cannot see because they're looking over it.

If you think about it, all these ideas are difficult to realize. But it's incredibly important the client realizes these things rather than just listens to you say them.

So how do you help a client realize these ideas for themself? You do so by asking questions: Do you think of your business as a business or do you have a nonprofit mindset when it comes to accomplishing your mission? What would happen if your entire staff understood how the company makes and spends money? What would happen if you dropped your least profitable products and allotted the marketing and sales energy you're currently using on those products to the products that are really making you money?

These questions are much more powerful than marching orders. If we say to a client, "Look, drop your bottom three products and instead use that energy to focus on your top three," the client will never realize the principle behind that action. If they don't realize the principle behind the action, they never develop the business acumen it takes to succeed over and over again. Your job as a coach is to turn your client into a business athlete that can succeed at the highest level, and to do that you will need to help them realize the principles behind the frameworks.

The point is this: As coaches, we don't teach as much as we help people realize certain truths for themselves. This, of course, changes our coaching conversations. We start asking more questions, we start telling more stories, we start affirming the indicators that they are beginning to understand what we are teaching.

CHARACTERISTIC FOUR: THEY CREATE A SAFE AND TRUSTING ENVIRONMENT

Beware of assuming you know what's going on in your client's business and life. Because we've had so many coaching conversations, we often start filling in the blanks based on experiences we've had with other clients. But when we fill in the blanks rather than dig deeper to find out what's really going on, our clients assume we aren't listening and as a result won't trust us.

Empathy matters for more reasons than just positioning yourself as a guide. Truly understanding and empathizing with your clients' pain will also create a safe and trusting environment. Actively listening and asking questions such as "I hear you saying that you feel betrayed by members of your team—is that right?" will ensure that you aren't assuming you know what's going on but rather are attempting to completely understand what your client is struggling with.

Once you truly understand your client's problem, it's also important to take a nonjudgmental position. If a client senses we hold them in judgment, the relationship is likely over. To create a trusting relationship, think of your work broken down as follows:

1. Listening, understanding, and verifying you understand your client's problem: 50 percent of your coaching work.

2. Affirming the client is not alone in their problem and that many others have experienced the same challenge: 40 percent of your coaching work.

3. Offering advice, frameworks, and playbooks that solve your client's problems: 10 percent of your coaching work.

If you remember that 90 percent of your job is to listen, understand, and "be with" your clients in their frustrations, the advice you give will actually be adopted, whereas if we don't create a safe environment, the coaching we give will mostly be ignored.

Finally, as it relates to gaining a client's trust, remember to always keep your confidentiality agreements and be loyal to those you coach.

CHARACTERISTIC FIVE: THEY AFFIRM THE TRANSFORMATION OF THEIR CLIENTS

At the end of many movies, after the hero has won the day, bloodied though they may be, the guide steps back into the story to affirm the transformation of the hero. For instance, Lionel, the drama teacher in Tom Hooper's Academy Award–winning movie, *The King's Speech*, tells King George that he will be a good king. Dr. Emmett Brown affirms the work Marty McFly does to save his family in *Back to the Future*. In the great sports film *Rudy*, a groundskeeper named Fortune offers encouragement and direction helping Rudy finally play in a game for Notre

Dame, then returns to affirm Rudy's transformation at the end of the movie.

All great stories are about the transformation of the hero from fearful to courageous, incompetent to competent, and even weak to strong. What's interesting about stories, though, is they acknowledge that heroes can't realize this transformation on their own.

> Heroes need to be told by a proven and trusted outside
> source that they have indeed changed.

As your client grows in business acumen and stature, affirm their changes. When you do so, you will find that they live into those changes and, usually only after you affirm them, begin to fully demonstrate the new traits they have developed.

In addition to affirming the client's transformation, celebrate their victories. When your client finally hits that revenue goal, write them a card or frame a memento and deliver it to them. Take them to dinner or buy them a gift. Many of the most accomplished people in the world are still looking for some kind of personal affirmation that acknowledges their accomplishments and transformation. Stopping to celebrate the victories your client has accomplished along with the transformation they have experienced will not only encourage your client, it will change the way they view themself and, as such, improve their lives forever.

There are, of course, a thousand more soft skills to discuss. The point of this chapter, though, was not to create a comprehensive list. Such an endeavor would be impossible. The point of the chapter is to stimulate some list making of your own.

Many coaches create their own top ten rules of coaching, and I think such a list is a good idea for all of us. A top ten list might look like this:

1. Never assume you know the client's problem.

2. Never assume your client understood your coaching.

3. Never break a client's trust.

4. Never make the story about you.

5. Be accountable to help the client find a win.

6. Demand engagement as part of the price of your coaching.

7. Be fully present in every coaching session.

8. Practice what you preach.

9. Apologize and correct yourself when you are wrong.

10. Affirm your client's transformation at every level of their growth.

Creating your own personal list of rules is a terrific way to remember the importance of soft skills and to follow through on them in every session. If you create the rules yourself, you will be more likely to own them and put them into practice. If you think about it, the list is really about who you are deciding to be as a human being: a person of good character. For that reason alone, a list like the one above is incredibly beneficial to any coach. Not only this, it's also a great assignment for your clients.

> As much as I've emphasized the importance of frameworks, playbooks, and an overall road map for your clients, let's not forget the soft skills.

When the frameworks and playbooks you offer are delivered from a trusted guide, they will be adhered to more completely, and as such will deliver the results your clients are looking for.

A Week in the Life of a Successful Business Coach

nce you take the eight steps I've laid out in this book, you will have the tools you need to grow a successful coaching business. Now, let's put all those steps together into a weekly routine.

What does a week in the life of a successful small business coach look like? It depends, of course. Some coaches are mostly retired, only tending to a few clients each week, and others are working on building a seven-figure coaching business.

For ease and clarity, I'll show you a week in the life of a coach somewhere in between. Let's say that our fictional coach, let's call him Sam, pivoted his career from the corporate world only a few years ago and is currently making about $256,000 as a small business coach. Sam used the Coach Builder Playbook to grow his business and achieved his $256,000 run rate within about thirty-six months. It was not easy but Sam kept working the system and continues to work just as hard to keep his coaching business strong and grow it further.

Sam isn't completely satisfied with the size of his business, but he likes where it's at only thirty-six months in and he likes where it's going. That said, how much time is the business costing Sam?

To show you what it costs Sam in terms of time, let's look at a "perfect week" from Sam's perspective. A "perfect week" is a week that, if repeated over and over, will ensure a person's success. The idea is to fully understand best practices and assign those practices to specific times on specific days and repeat them in order to achieve the best results.

What you will notice about the "perfect week" is that nearly every aspect of the product and sales funnel I have discussed in this book is being put into play as the week plays out; thus our coach continues to build his business.

If you're wondering what a perfect week in your life might look like a year or so after you start your coaching business, it might look something like this:

MONDAY: DELIVER COACHING

On Monday, Sam is focused on delivering coaching collateral to his clients. Because Sam is rested going into Monday, he schedules most of his coaching for Monday and Tuesday, then the tasks he needs to do to grow his business for Wednesday, and finally creative work (along with extra coaching) on Thursday and Friday.

Remember, this is an example of a perfect week in Sam's life. Of course, no week goes perfectly, but by defining the perfect week, Sam has a standard to aim toward.

7:00 A.M. TO 8:00 A.M.

Family: Sam spends the first hour of his week with his family. The kids get a much better start to their week if Dad is around, so he gets up and starts cooking breakfast early. After cooking, Sam, his wife, and children sit around the breakfast table and share what they're most excited about in the coming week. Sam makes sure all of his children are affirmed and encouraged before they leave the house.

8:00 A.M. TO 10:00 A.M.

Workout: Rather than jumping into work first thing Monday morning, Sam heads to the gym where he swims laps for an hour. Mostly, though, Sam uses the time in the pool to meditate on the coming coaching sessions.

10:00 A.M. TO 12:00 P.M.

Small Business Mastermind One: Sam runs two Small Business Mastermind groups (his high-level mastermind), each with ten small business owners who have signed on for the six-month experience. (He also runs a Small Business Community Group as an entry-level community, but they do not meet until the end of the week.) For his mastermind participants, he has already sent out a video and an assignment early Monday morning so they should already have watched the video and reviewed the assignment. Sam spends ninety minutes on a Zoom call with his first mastermind making sure they understood that week's assignment and then walks them through the accompanying exercise. He also checks up with his group on last week's assignment to make sure they are fully executing the exercises so they see the best results. After the ninety-minute session wraps up, Sam spends thirty minutes looking through his clients' work and makes encouraging and helpful notes they can use to better implement the frameworks.

12:00 P.M. TO 2:00 P.M.

Lunch: Sam uses Monday lunch to get together with potential clients. He tries to schedule at least one lunch per week with somebody who has questions about his coaching services. After the lunch, he will send the future client a link to MyBusinessReport .com and then follow up with them later to review their assessment and inform them about the various coaching opportunities he offers. Often, these lunches result in a new client joining his mastermind group or even a one-on-one coaching engagement.

2:00 P.M. TO 4:00 P.M.

Small Business Mastermind Two: Sam conducts his second mastermind, taking the group through the exact same exercises and questions as the morning group. Sam arranges both his masterminds to start and end on the same days so he only has to prepare for one video and exercise each week.

4:00 P.M. TO 5:00 P.M.

First One-on-One Coaching Session: Sam conducts the first of four one-on-one coaching exchanges for the week. These one-on-one sessions start off with a five-hour on-ramping session that takes place in person and then continue with two one-hour sessions each month. The one-hour sessions take place on Zoom, allowing Sam to coach clients anywhere in the country.

5:00 P.M. TO 9:00 P.M.

Family Time.

TUESDAY:
CONTINUE TO DELIVER COACHING

Tuesday is a continuation of coaching delivery, except on Tuesday Sam only schedules one-on-one clients. Because each of Sam's one-on-one clients only meet with him twice each month, he can conduct one one-on-one session on Monday and three on Tuesday and coach four total one-on-one clients per week. Conducting the sessions at the same time each week allows Sam to enjoy a predictable routine that ensures he is able to prepare for and give the best possible coaching advice without becoming overwhelmed.

7:00 A.M. TO 8:00 A.M.
Family: Sam spends the first hour of his day with his family.

8:00 A.M. TO 10:00 A.M.
Workout: Sam heads to the gym where he swims laps for an hour. Sam uses the time in the pool to think through the coming coaching sessions.

10:00 A.M. TO 11:00 A.M.
Second One-on-One Coaching Session: Sam conducts his second one-on-one coaching session. Each of his one-on-one clients is at a different place in his custom-created program, but because these are individualized sessions, Sam can easily help them overcome their current challenges. Often, Sam will request to meet with the client's entire leadership team so they can fully engage whichever framework or playbook they are working on that week.

11 A.M. TO 11:30 A.M.

Take a Break and Prepare: Sam takes half-hour breaks between coaching sessions so he is sure to be ready and present for each client.

11:30 A.M. TO 12:30 P.M.

Third One-on-One Coaching Session: Sam delivers his third one-on-one coaching session of the week.

12:30 P.M. TO 2:30 P.M.

Lunch: Sam takes a lunch break, often getting together with another future client.

2:30 P.M. TO 3:30 P.M.

Fourth One-on-One Coaching Session: Sam conducts his fourth and final one-on-one coaching session of the week, concluding all of his coaching sessions. In only two days, Sam has provided coaching to two Small Business Masterminds and four of his eight one-on-one clients.

3:30 P.M. TO 4:00 P.M.

Review and Prepare for Next Week: Sam sends notes or emails to clients that he has marked for follow-up, getting them the information and help they may have requested. He reviews the videos and exercises his masterminds will be going through the following week and makes notes he will review tomorrow during his prep session.

4:00 P.M. TO 9:00 P.M.
Family Time.

WEDNESDAY:
MARKETING AND BUSINESS BUILDING

7:00 A.M. TO 10:00 A.M.

Family Time: Sam skips the gym on Wednesday and spends a little more time with his family.

10:00 A.M. TO 12:00 P.M.

Marketing and Client Acquisition Review: Sam reviews his personal CRM to see who is opening and responding to his automated email campaigns. He will need twenty more mastermind participants after his current masterminds conclude. He sees that twelve future clients are responding to his mastermind on-ramping sequence so he makes a note to follow up with those clients after lunch.

12:00 P.M. TO 2:00 P.M.

Lunch: Sam either has lunch with a future client, a friend, or a family member or he gets some much-needed alone time.

2:00 P.M. TO 4:00 P.M.

Follow Up: Sam calls each of his most interested leads to let them know about the next Small Business Community Group or mastermind opportunity. Again, each mastermind runs for six months, and so the closer the calendar gets to the start of the next mastermind, the more commitments Sam needs to keep his coaching slots full. One-on-one coaching is based on an open-ended timeline and so Sam doesn't worry about filling those spaces. As soon as one of his one-on-one coaching clients drops out, there are plenty of current and former Small Business

Community Group or mastermind clients ready and waiting to take their spot so Sam does not have to worry about marketing and lead generation for the one-on-one coaching product.

4:00 P.M. TO 5:00 P.M.
Follow Up: Sam follows up with any highly qualified leads by sending them a personal note along with a copy of a business book he thinks might help them. He makes sure all of these leads are on his mastermind nurture email list.

5:00 P.M. TO 9:00 P.M.
Family Time.

THURSDAY:
WORKSHOP DELIVERY, SMALL BUSINESS COMMUNITY GROUP MEETINGS, OR REST AND RECOVERY

7:00 A.M. TO 8:00 A.M.
Family: Sam spends the first hour of his day with his family.

8:00 A.M. TO 5:00 P.M.
Workshop Delivery: Sam either delivers a workshop to a small group of leaders or, if there is no workshop scheduled, Sam takes the day off to go to the gym, play golf, or spend time with friends and family. The kinds of workshops Sam delivers are management and productivity workshops, sales trainings, or guiding principles workshops. Sam delivers about six workshops each year.

OR

8:00 A.M. TO 5:00 P.M.

Small Business Community Group Delivery: If Sam does not have a workshop, he can easily facilitate between one and four Small Business Community Groups, his flagship, entry-level community from which he generates leads for most of his other products. These groups are more informal and require less preparation and Sam enjoys them because they tend to be fun.

FRIDAY: COACHING PREPARATION

7:00 A.M. TO 8:00 A.M.

Family: Sam spends the first hour of his day with his family.

8:00 A.M. TO 12:00 P.M.

Preparation: Sam spends his morning preparing for his next two masterminds and his next four one-on-one coaching sessions. He reviews his client notes, sending them encouraging emails and writing down thoughts for reflection to bring up in the masterminds that will take place the following week.

12:00 P.M. TO 9:00 P.M.

Rest and Recovery: Sam takes half the day on Friday to run errands, go for walks, play golf, spend time with family, and *not* think about work. It's his rhythm of work and rest that keeps him sharp and focused during his coaching sessions.

WEEKEND: FUN, FRIENDS, AND FAMILY

Sam does not do work on the weekends, saving himself up for the strongest possible Monday and Tuesday when most of his coaching takes place.

NOTES ON THE PERFECT WEEK

The perfect week rarely goes as planned, of course, but Sam always keeps it as close to perfect as possible. He does not reschedule his clients based on their schedules. If a client misses a session, they agree to pay for the session anyway. This allows Sam to keep his schedule as routine and predictable as possible. Interruptions such as family vacations and out-of-town workshops occasionally disrupt Sam, but he knows if he schedules those workshops on Thursdays or Fridays, he can get his preparation done on the plane or in a hotel room somewhere. Still, the harder Sam fights to stick to his perfect week, the faster his coaching business grows.

It's a good idea for all of us in the coaching business to sit down with a calendar and create a perfect week. The main reason it matters, though, is to let us know when our lives are becoming too chaotic. And, as you know, our lives becoming too chaotic usually happens when we say "yes" to too many opportunities. One of your clients wants you to vacation with him on his new yacht? Super tough to pass up, and yet it kills one of your perfect weeks. That might have to be a solid *no*, especially if you are still building your coaching practice. Yachts are for people who have multimillion-dollar coaching businesses, not those who are building a multimillion-dollar coaching business.

If we really want to grow a successful coaching business, we need to figure out how to get all the foundational actions it takes to grow our businesses done every week, week after week, and writing down our perfect schedule is the best way to make sure we get close to that.

WHAT IF YOU WANT TO GROW YOUR COACHING BUSINESS BEYOND A SOLO OPERATION?

Let's talk next about what you should do if you would like to build your coaching business into a seven-figure agency or even beyond. If you're willing to do the very hard work, what work should you do?

I've laid out an advanced growth plan in the next chapter. If you are looking to build a full coaching agency, and even elevate yourself as a thought leader by building a personal platform, I believe the step-by-step process I lay out in the next chapter will be helpful.

How to Scale Your Coaching Business to Seven Figures and Beyond

I t's certainly possible to grow a seven-figure coaching business, but before we get into how to do it, I have a question: Do you really want to?

To scale your coaching business, you'll have to bring on people, and when you bring on people that means you have to hire and fire, create detailed job descriptions, manage the people you hire, create systems and processes so that workflows are effective, and so on. The bottom line is this: When you scale, life gets complicated.

Most of us become small business coaches because we love working with small business owners, but as you scale, you'll find you won't be working with very many small business owners anymore. Instead, you will be in meetings with your team, with the coaches who coach under you, with your accountant, with your marketing agent, and probably with a lawyer or two along the way.

Nobody gets into business because they want to run a business. We get into business because we love our customers and our products and the transformation that happens when those two entities collide. When you scale your operation, though, you will be one step removed from the close contact with clients you originally signed up for.

I open this chapter with these concerns because I believe they're worth considering. To be candid, I'm hoping to talk some of you out of scaling your operation. Why? Because scaling your coaching business from the low six figures to the low seven figures and beyond could decrease rather than increase your quality of life.

WHAT ARE THE PERSONAL COSTS INVOLVED IN BUILDING A SEVEN-FIGURE COACHING BUSINESS?

The reality is, if you scale your coaching business, some of the time you currently spend with family will need to be spent keeping your coaching business aloft. The time you currently spend reading books may need to be spent writing one. The time you currently spend playing golf may need to be spent speaking in front of groups of small business owners, inviting them to join one of your coaching groups.

Of course, once your machine is built, you will be able to manage the machine with a limited amount of time, but don't be fooled: Building the machine itself will take a great deal of sacrifice. Even after it's built you will find it needs more time than the "run a business from your bubble bath" books lead you to believe.

In addition to the time it's going to cost you, it's going to cost you worry, too. Whatever stress you currently feel as a coach will be compounded. If you've ever wondered where your next client is going to come from, imagine wondering where your next three clients are coming from because you now have three coaches coaching under you, and they all need new clients. And, by the way, those coaches didn't sign up to do marketing; they signed up to coach, so they are not going to help much with client acquisition.

If you are making good money and enjoy a healthy work-life balance and are fulfilled with your life as a small business coach, don't bother scaling your coaching practice into a small coaching agency. Just keep doing what you're doing and enjoy your life.

However, there are a small number of people reading this book who roll their eyes at everything I've just written. It's not that they don't agree with me; it's just that they could care less what growing a seven-figure coaching business is going to cost them. They are driven and they want to accomplish their dream. They are convinced they can grow a coaching business while staying responsible to their family and friends, and they aren't interested in picking up any new hobbies or even thinking about retirement. If that's you, keep reading.

It's my view that the only coaches who should scale their coaching business into the millions of dollars are the coaches who have no choice. What I mean by having no choice is they are driven by an ambition that isn't going to go away no matter how many people lecture them about work-life balance. Sure, they care about work-life balance, but they know they can self-correct when the time comes. What they really want, more than anything else, is to build something they are proud of, something that changes people's lives, including their own.

If you want to build a seven-figure coaching business, what follows is a playbook.

The playbook is scalable and you can use it to grow as large as you want. Here's a warning, though: The larger you get, the less time you are going to have for yourself. The truth is, I gave up nearly all hobbies years ago. In order to be a good husband and father and also run a business, there was little room for anything else. I bought season tickets to Nashville Soccer Club so that, at least ten times each year, I could sit with three friends and watch a sport as a way of batching outside interests. Those games and an annual fishing trip are about it. I don't play golf, I don't have a pilot's license, I don't sit in the backyard and paint landscapes. This isn't to say I'm not happy. I am happy and grateful for my life. However, most of my community, my interests, and my passions (all of which I still have) revolve around writing, speaking, and coaching. I like it that much.

I love building my coaching business and I love the impact it is having on clients. I am able to be present as a husband and father and also impact the world, which is a life I'm grateful for. On that one fishing trip I take each year, I take enough pictures to spread them out on Instagram making it look like I have a hobby, but truly my hobby is just work right now. And I believe this is appropriate for the season I am in. If you want to build the business of your dreams, you can't just dream—you have to wake up and do the work.

That said, what is the work?

THE SEVEN-FIGURE COACHING
BUSINESS PLAYBOOK

I am going to break down the steps to build a seven-figure coaching business into five hiring decisions and five job descriptions to go along with those five hiring decisions.

I like breaking down the steps into hiring decisions because the reality is you can't build a coaching agency alone. At each level of growth, you will need to hire certain people to fulfill certain roles. I also believe there are a thousand ways to build a coaching business and we can all take a different path, but what we will all have in common are these hiring decisions. To build a coaching agency is to build a team. You can build that team slowly or quickly (I recommend going slow) but the specific team I will lay out for you will give you the best chance of success.

In the end, your coaching business will run like a small company comprised of administrative help, a marketing department, a sales department, a content department, and of course a coaching department. Those departments can then scale as large as you want them to scale.

My friend Howard Partridge down in Houston has built a terrific coaching business that revolves around his own books, live events, small groups, and even digital products. Amazingly, Howard also runs his own rug-cleaning business on the side, practicing everything he preaches to his own community of small business owners in his own successful small business.

Even more amazingly, Howard still finds time to be fully present with his grandchildren and, once in a while, finds himself on a beach with a mai tai in his hand, so there's hope for the rest of us.

WHAT DOES A SEVEN-FIGURE COACHING BUSINESS LOOK LIKE?

Before we get into the step-by-step playbook, let's talk about what our coaching agency might look like after it's been built. Here's how Howard's business works: He hosts one large event every year. The event runs for three days. He does most of the speaking and teaching, but the coaches who coach under him also get time on the stage. He also brings in guest speakers.

This event helps Howard create a large community of small business owners who know and look out for each other.

Howard then has multiple small groups that meet twice each month. The coaches that coach under Howard lead those small groups.

Howard sets one elite small group aside to lead himself, and this top-tier small group also has their own retreat that he leads.

Howard writes books (again, Howard Partridge is his name if you want to look him up) and speaks at outside events, bringing in a little royalty and honorarium revenue, too.

Howard's coaching business brings in revenue well into seven figures and he's still growing.

This may sound like an easy lift, but look back at all Howard is doing and think about the logistical necessities to pull it off. He needs a team of coaches, which means he needs somebody to help recruit, hire, and train those coaches. He is running several events, which means he needs an event coordinator. He needs consistent lead acquisition, which means he needs somebody to handle his marketing and sales. Then he needs to create coaching content and meet with his clients personally, which means he needs somebody to help manage his schedule so he has plenty of time to be creative and present.

THE SEVEN-FIGURE COACHING BUSINESS HIRING PLAN AND TIMELINE

Again, your seven-figure playbook is captured here in the form of a hiring plan. Consider each hire a step in the process of building your agency. I recommend only making the next hire when the previous hire has settled into their role and is producing profitable results, allowing you to increase your rainy-day fund and invest in more labor.

Each hire will have a specific job description and as such will take the tasks assigned to them off of your plate. In a small coaching agency, each team member has several responsibilities. But as the team grows, each job description includes fewer and fewer objectives. By the time you've built a seven-figure coaching business, each team member should be thought of as a specialist dialed in on their specific role within the business.

With that, here's a seven-figure playbook in the form of a hiring plan:

LEVEL ONE:
Solo Coaching Business

The previous chapters of this book are designed to help you build a terrific solo coaching business, which, I believe, is the hardest stage of building a coaching business. Getting a rocket off the launching pad takes much more energy than whirling it around the earth once in orbit.

Your primary concerns as you build your solo coaching business should revolve around defining your products, building your CRM, delivering great coaching, and retaining existing clients while on-ramping new clients at or above your rate of attrition.

As fast as you can, however, you will want to hire a virtual assistant. For now, though, let's look at a job description for you, the solo coach hoping to scale your business. You are, after all, the foundation on which your coaching agency will be built.

Of course, this person does not need to be hired because, well, you are this person. You are a solo coach. Nevertheless, a good job description for you will provide clarity about what, exactly, your responsibilities are as a solo coach.

Solo Coach Job Description

JOB OVERVIEW: A motivated and experienced coach who will work with small business owners to transform their leadership ability, clarify their marketing messages, help them close more sales, optimize their product offerings, manage their teams, and manage their cash flow all with the focus of growing each client's overall revenue.

■ **RESPONSIBILITIES:**

- Represent or create a line of coaching products that help small business owners overcome their primary challenges.
- Create and manage a CRM to acquire new clients and retain existing clients.
- Create the marketing materials necessary to grow your coaching business, including landing pages, lead generators, nurture emails, and sales emails.

- Conduct coaching sessions in the form of masterminds and one-on-one coaching.
- Conduct workshops to help teams improve their guiding principles, marketing messages, sales, and management abilities.
- Practice empathy and understanding so small business owners do not feel alone in their challenges.
- Curate and shepherd a community of small business owners.

■ **REQUIREMENTS:**

- Five years of experience either working with small business leaders or running a small business.
- Strong knowledge of the frameworks and playbooks necessary to run a small business.
- Good problem-solving skills.
- Patience and empathy with small business owners who are under perpetual pressure.
- Ability to work independently and stay motivated to deliver results within their own business and for their clients.
- Good, trustworthy people skills.
- Motivated to grow their small coaching business.

LEVEL TWO:

Solo Coach with a Virtual Assistant

As your solo coaching business grows, your first hire should be a virtual assistant. Any coach who is engaging more than ten clients should consider hiring a virtual assistant to free up their time to do what they enjoy doing most, which is likely coaching. A virtual assistant can assist you for as few as ten hours each week or as many as forty, making this a great first hire because they can scale with you while keeping costs down.

My favorite virtual assistant company is BELAY Solutions out of Atlanta. I've worked with BELAY to help them understand the needs of a small business coach and so they are already aware of your needs to build and manage CRMs, manage your schedule, manage your correspondence, and so on. Regardless of the virtual assistant company you go with, you are looking for somebody who has plug-and-play solutions to immediately lessen your workload and allow you to focus more exclusively on the parts of your job that allow you the greatest impact and greatest enjoyment.

COACH'S STORY

I was a "solo coach" for years until that light bulb moment hit me and clearly said, "Girl, you are going to burn out if you keep this pace up!" I knew that the underlying issue was control. I didn't believe anyone could do things as well as I could. But once I gave in and hired a virtual assistant, she became another set of hands and an even better mind than I had for process-driven tasks. Using Don's process of creating a clear job description and identifying the tasks that were ideal to be outsourced, I found and hired the perfect virtual assistant for my practice. Having her onboard is similar to the process of cloning myself! She took on the things that I had no business doing, and it freed me up to do the things that are within my wheelhouse. I'm now ready to hire a second coach and expand the practice even further. None of which could have been done if I hadn't followed the process to hire my first virtual assistant!

—SUSAN TRUMPLER,
business coach since 2013

The following job description will work for an assistant at about thirty hours each week but parts of the job description can be excluded or added based on your specific needs and budget.

As you read the job description for your first hire, a virtual assistant, know that you are a solo operation and there is not much of a line between your personal life and your professional responsibilities. Your virtual assistant, then, should also take on some of your personal tasks as a way of freeing up more of your time and energy.

Virtual Assistant Job Description

JOB OVERVIEW: Assist a small business coach in the daily execution of their personal and professional responsibilities so they have more time to devote to their friends, family, and clients.

■   **RESPONSIBILITIES:**

- Schedule: Manage their boss's schedule including their personal and professional appointments by utilizing software applications such as Google Calendar, Keap, and Business Made Simple's Flight Plan.

- Work-Life Balance: Help their boss manage their personal priorities, including time with family, vacations, date nights, gift giving, scheduling haircuts, subscriptions and memberships, home maintenance, and any repeatable tasks that will free up their boss's time.

- Correspondence: Review their boss's email and respond to inquiries based on previously agreed-upon responses. Decrease the amount of correspondence coming to their boss by only forwarding pertinent emails. Follow up with their boss to make sure important correspondence is not dropped.

- Manage CRM: Manage their boss's CRM to make sure potential clients are entered into the system, existing clients are put into the right nurture campaigns, and all copy, links, and landing pages are up to date and functional.

- Billing: Send invoices to clients and make sure they are up to date on their coaching payments.

- Expenses: Track all expenses for the business and manage the correspondence with the accountant.

- Project Management: Initiate, manage, and fully execute all projects, including event coordination, media, and production responsibilities, along with personal projects such as vacations and home management.

- Client Interaction: Build positive relationships with their boss's clients by following up with them after masterminds or one-on-one coaching sessions.

Make sure each client has what they need to execute any homework assigned to them by their coach.

■ REQUIREMENTS:

- Five years of experience working with solopreneurs to help them organize their life and work.
- Competency with software that manages schedules, email, project management, and CRM functions.
- Able to anticipate needs and challenges before they arise.
- Terrific people skills for interacting with coaching clients.
- Professional business writing capability.
- Strong project management skills.
- Ability to work and contribute positively to a team.

■

Regardless of whether you want to build a large coaching agency, I recommend getting a personal assistant. You will find that the work the assistant takes off your shoulders allows you to make more than enough in added revenue to cover their salary.

LEVEL THREE:

A Virtual Assistant and a Second Coach

As you build your email list you will also be building your personal platform, and your coaching clients will increase. You, personally, will likely still be leading masterminds and one-on-one coaching along with workshops, but you will also find that, after a year or two, you may resent the fact that you've built a business that requires you to constantly be in the room (or on Zoom) with clients.

Your virtual assistant will be handling more and more of the marketing load and also scheduling and corresponding with clients. At this point you may want to consider bringing on a coach who can take on at least four more entry-level community groups or second-tier masterminds, that is two every six months, each of which includes about ten clients.

At this level, the overall organization will consist of two coaches (you are still one of them) and a virtual assistant.

Your second coach (same job description as previously listed above) should be able to coach forty clients per year as long as you can keep the quantity of qualified leads and recurring clients at an elevated level. Each client should be paying around $250 per month for an entry-level community group or $5,000 for a six-month mastermind, allowing the second coach to deliver about $200,000 worth of revenue per year. Because the coach will not have to do their own marketing and because their coaching will be limited to the mastermind hours, they will not be working full-time and so you can likely pay them around $85,000 per year, which, of course, leaves the rest as profit.

Add to this that each new coach, once their coaching hours are filled, is increasing the chances of clients buying products that are higher on your product ladder, including workshops and elite masterminds.

The challenge, of course, will involve getting forty new clients per year to sign up to fill four more coaches' schedules. To accomplish this, your CRM engine will need to be operating efficiently enough to carry the lead generation and customer acquisition load. That said, if more of your time is now freed to create lead generators, deliver keynote speeches, host business breakfasts and lunches, and perhaps even record a podcast or helpful YouTube and social media collateral, and your virtual assistant is doing a good job managing the CRM that assimilates and communicates to the new leads you are bringing in, your coaching agency should be off to a good start and your top-line revenue should be north of $500,000, well on your way to your first million-dollar year.

LEVEL FOUR:
A Virtual Assistant, a Second Coach, and a Community Events Coordinator

At any point, you can pause the growth of your coaching business and enjoy its current stage (along with the community you have created), but if you want to keep growing, it's time to start holding retreats, meet-ups, and perhaps an annual summit.

Holding events is an enormous part of Howard Partridge's strategy down in Texas. He holds an annual retreat in a banquet room in Houston as a way of creating a larger community, then the small business owners who attend his annual event are offered the opportunity to get into small groups led by his coaching team.

Adding an event strategy doesn't have to stop at an annual summit, either. You can also add monthly breakfasts, regional meet-ups (led by your second coach), a weekly Zoom Q&A, and even holiday parties.

Our research shows that coaching clients don't sign up for coaching because of community, but they tend to stick around because of the community they've discovered so it's important to see community as a retention play.

If you're going to add events to your offering, you will need an events coordinator. Here is a job description for the person you'd need to fill that position:

Event Coordinator Job Description

JOB OVERVIEW: Plan, organize, and execute events that create a community for small business owners involved in a coaching community. These events will include workshops, conferences, seminars, breakfasts, webinars, Zoom Q&A calls, and holiday parties.

■ **RESPONSIBILITIES:**

- Strategize: Consider the types of events that will grow a community of small business owners and develop a timeline for each event.
- Coordinate: Work with all vendors to coordinate successful events.
- Manage: Manage the events as they happen so they run smoothly and are enjoyable for our clients.
- Budget: Create and work within a budget.
- Revenue Creation: Find ways to generate further revenue creation through our event strategy.
- Measure: Measure event attendance and satisfaction to generate accurate data about what is working and what is not.
- Inform: Inform the team about best practices in our event strategy.

- Promote: Work with the team to create a promotion strategy so that each event is well attended. Measure the success of each strategy.

■ **REQUIREMENTS:**

- Five years previous experience in the event-planning space.
- Excellent project management skills, including the ability to manage multiple projects at once.
- Strong written and verbal communication skills.
- Ability to work collaboratively with a variety of team members, clients, and stakeholders, including coaches, vendors, and event attendees.
- Strong attention to detail, especially as it relates to managing an event budget.
- Ability to work and contribute positively to a team.

LEVEL FIVE:
A Virtual Assistant, a Second Coach, a Community Events Coordinator, and a Content Creator/Manager

As your coaching community grows, your primary challenge will be filling all the coaching small groups and events. To do this, you are going to need a content strategy. To create and maintain a buzz about all you offer, you and your organization will want to produce incredibly helpful information small business owners can use to accomplish their objectives.

Because you will be running the organization as well as delivering coaching, you will likely not have time to create the kind of content necessary to fill your events. This is where a content creator/manager can play a critical role.

Your content manager can schedule a weekly meeting with you to capture new social media content, giving you prompts and ideas you can expand upon in posts and videos. They can create content that will allow you to build a YouTube channel while also creating keynote decks your coaches can deliver during webinars, keynotes, workshops, breakout sessions, and so forth.

Your content manager can also help you better understand what clients are looking for. They can conduct a quarterly survey to query interests and then recommend a content direction for you that will elevate engagement.

The goal of your content strategy should be to deepen and expand your reach so that your coaching products spread further and your reputation increases attention and trust.

Content Manager Job Description

JOB OVERVIEW: Manage all aspects of our media presence, including social media, copywriting, and content creation, YouTube video strategy and creation, keynote and webinar content creation, and more.

■ **RESPONSIBILITIES:**

- Strategize: Develop and implement a comprehensive media strategy to promote all of our small business coaching products.
- Curate: Curate relevant, topical content to be shared by our coaches on all platforms.

- Measure and Refine: Monitor our social media statistics along with social media trends to surmise best practices, allowing our content strategy to effectively grow our platforms.
- Keynotes: Develop keynotes coaches can share on webinars as well as live keynotes they can deliver at our own events and the various speaking events in which they are invited to attend.
- Social Media Growth: Strategize and help grow our social media platforms for the overall agency and specific coaches.
- YouTube: Create and execute a strategy that will allow our coaching agency to extend to and grow on YouTube.

■ **REQUIREMENTS:**

- Extremely strong written and verbal communication skills.
- Knowledge of best practices on all social media platforms.
- Excellent organization and project management capabilities.
- Three years of experience in content creation for an organization.
- Experience managing social media for an outside client.
- Experience in graphic design, including all current software requirements to build and sustain a visual brand.
- Ability to work and contribute positively to a team.

LEVEL SIX:

A Virtual Assistant, a Second or Third Coach, a Community Events Coordinator, a Content Creator/ Manager, and an Operations Manager

Congratulations. If you have risen to level six, you have a seven-figure coaching agency. In fact, there's a good chance you are making multiple millions in your top-line revenue. You also have a terrific community of clients and a staff that is starting to feel like a family. At least this is my hope. It's certainly a realistic possibility.

The question to ask yourself now is, how much do you want to be personally involved in the day-to-day management of the business itself? Would you like to be semi-retired, sitting on a beach taking calls to answer questions from your staff? Would you like to be writing books, creating the content that fuels the overall coaching community? Would you like to be creating a media presence on YouTube or social media that feeds the agency?

The truth is, your entrepreneurial talent may be best utilized outside a manager's role and it might be time to hire an operator who can run your coaching agency.

At the top of most successful small businesses there are often three distinct personalities. Those personalities are:

The Artist: The Artist obsesses about product and product creation. They obsess about customer experience, brand quality, and alignment with the values that drive their vision forward.

The Operator: The Operator obsesses about the people and processes that are going to grow the business. They obsess about measuring the methods and success of the processes they use and managing the people in the organization so they are equipped to deliver the best results.

The Entrepreneur: The Entrepreneur turns their habit of attention to revenue creation and growth. They love to take the products the Artist creates and monetize those products.

As you read that list, you likely found yourself identifying with the Artist or the Entrepreneur. If this is the case, know that managing the day-to-day operations of your coaching business is going to feel draining to you. An operations person is unique in their habit of attention. They do not want to build the machine; they want to manage the machine. If you've built a machine, then it's time to find somebody who can manage it well.

Your point of contact with the agency, once you fill this position, will be your Operator. While you will certainly interact with everybody on your team, the Operator will now execute your vision using their excellent skills organizing both people and processes.

Again, when you hire an Operator, you are hiring somebody to run your company, freeing you up to do the work you do best growing the business or, perhaps, to work less and enjoy more time with friends, family, and hobbies.

Your Operator can be given the title of CEO, President, COO, Director of Operations, or Operations Manager. The title hardly matters. What matters is they run your company so you can be free to either start taking more time off, or continue to grow the business by spending more time in your areas of competency.

Director of Operations Job Description

JOB OVERVIEW: Oversee the day-to-day operations of a small business coaching agency. Manage the people, processes, and finances that cause the agency to grow while maintaining the quality of our services to clients.

■ **RESPONSIBILITIES:**

- Policies and Procedures: Develop and implement the policies and procedures that allow our team to work at peak productivity and effectiveness.
- Finance: Develop and manage our budgets, forecasting, and reporting so that our agency is profitable and sound.
- Administrative: Manage our HR, IT, and facilities.
- Client Satisfaction: Maintain a close relationship with key clients to ensure the most satisfactory delivery of our coaching products.
- Collaborate: Work with the CEO to deliver the best possible coaching, which will include speaking into the overall strategy, content creation, timeline, and release processes.
- Future-casting: Help guide our agency by staying on top of industry trends and best practices, installing new policies and procedures so that we become and remain leaders in the small business coaching industry.

■ **QUALIFICATIONS:**

- Five years or more of experience in operations management.

- Experience managing the seven-figure budget of a service-based company.
- Proven success running a management and productivity playbook.
- Strong organizational and time-management skills.
- Proven ability to motivate and inspire a team.
- The ability to work calmly under pressure.
- Experience with the software necessary to run our organization, including Keynote, Keap, Slack, Microsoft Office, and so on.

LEVEL SEVEN:
A Virtual Assistant, a Second or Third Coach, a Community Events Coordinator, a Content Creator/ Manager, an Operations Manager, and a Revenue Director

As your Operator settles in and you become comfortable with them running your small business, and as the business demonstrates it can continue to operate or even grow under their leadership, you are likely heading toward $10 million or more in annual revenue. At this stage you will have already considered and perhaps even hired more coaches and administrative help. Your small agency may have as many as fifteen full-time team members and various virtual assistants and freelancers. You are truly running a successful coaching agency now and hopefully your work-life balance is strong.

If you want to continue growing your agency, though, your next and likely final hire will be a Revenue Director. If you are the Artist and your Director of Operations is the Operator, the only person you may be missing from your leadership team is the Entrepreneur. To move beyond $10 million you are going to need somebody whose full-time job is to strategize about how the agency can make more money.

The entrepreneur-minded position you are looking for can be given the title Revenue Director, Chief Revenue Officer, or some other title that reflects their primary responsibility: maximize revenue.

Here is a sample job description for a Revenue Director:

Revenue Director Job Description

JOB OVERVIEW: A highly motivated, results-driven Revenue Director for a growing small business coaching agency with the focused intent to double our current revenue. Our Revenue Director will be responsible for maximizing profitability by increasing revenue and reducing costs in all areas of the business.

■ **RESPONSIBILITIES:**

- Strategy: Develop and implement revenue-generating strategies with the stated objective to double our overall revenue.
- Manage: Build and develop high-functioning sales and marketing teams.
- Measure: Develop and implement real-time ways of measuring our marketing and sales efforts using our CRM and other software and services.
- Collaborate: Unite our marketing, sales, executive team, and customer service departments so they operate as one effective force.

- Client Satisfaction: Work with the CEO and content team to strategize and release products that are in-demand, profitable, and effective for our clients.
- Hit Our Goals: Help us hit our goals and celebrate our successes. Create and sustain a culture of winning.

■ QUALIFICATIONS:

- Experience: Ten or more years of experience in a sales, marketing, or other revenue-generating position, preferably in a coaching, consulting, or content-creation agency.
- Goal-Oriented: Proven experience driving revenue growth and hitting stated goals.
- Creativity: Proven creativity developing and installing new products into a product offering.
- Sales Optimization: Experience developing sales pipelines and helping sales and marketing teams close all gaps in client acquisition and conversion.
- Management: Excellent internal and external communication skills that prevent and disarm workplace drama.
- Negotiation: Proven ability to negotiate critical deals on our behalf.
- Sales: Proven ability to sell to key stakeholders.

BUILD AND REFINE
AND THEN REFINE AGAIN

When you make all the hires I've laid out in this chapter, you've built an incredible coaching business. This will be a massive accomplishment that required intention, focus, humility, and drive.

From here, sustaining your healthy coaching agency will require a ritual of refinement and then refinement again. You will experience staff and client churn and will need to refine both your culture and business strategy to minimize that churn. You will encounter the need for new and fresh content, better events, new digital strategies, and real-time navigation of economic and cultural disruptions.

To lead through these dynamics, you will want to install a rhythm of review and refinement. Your Operator can help you with this, but essentially you will want to ask questions that allow you to make and keep the business strong. Some of those questions are:

- How can we refine and improve our lead generation strategies?

- How can we improve our post-acquisition marketing strategies?

- How can we increase our conversion metrics?

- How can we improve our coaching small groups?

- How can we improve our upsell coaching offers?

- How can we improve our overall coaching community-building efforts?

- How can we improve our internal culture?

The point is this: After you have created a level of dependability in your operations, what's next is a never-ending improvement on those operations.

Once you are in this final stage of review and refinement, congratulations once again. You may have even built a coaching agency worth selling, which will finally give you the financial freedom you've been working so hard to attain. And even if you don't sell your coaching agency, you can go to work every day knowing you know how to build a successful small business at the highest level, thus reinforcing your competency (and reputation) as a small business coach.

If you've read this book and are filled with hope, I'm glad. Thousands of people just like you have built successful coaching businesses, so it's certainly possible for you, too. The global executive coaching industry is said to produce over $9 billion of revenue each year and it continues to grow. The world needs more coaches and I hope you become one of them.

Conclusion

The Point Is Transformation

I f you are worried you don't have what it takes to build a coaching business, you're worried because your fears are probably grounded in reality. How can you have what it takes to build a coaching business if you've never built one? In fact, it's only after you build a coaching business that you will know how it's done. The truth is, though, I don't currently know how to build a bookshelf but I could figure it out, and then I'd know how to build a bookshelf and could even teach somebody else to do it.

If you're feeling a little insecure about growing a coaching business, that's okay. We all feel insecure until we become competent. For you, competency is around the corner.

If you have succeeded in business and believe you can help people experience success for themselves, you have an excellent foundation on which to build a coaching business. Not only that, but the playbook contained in this book is all you need to start leveraging your experience into a profitable coaching career. All you have to do is take action. Competency and confidence will only follow action. You can't dream competency into existence. You just have to get moving. And if you move, you will transform, I promise.

One of the reasons stories are so fulfilling is because of the transformation the hero experiences after their journey. In a story, the hero sets out as a clumsy, scared, and ill-equipped protagonist and by the end they are agile, fearless, and competent. That is what's going to happen to you if you follow the steps in the Coach Builder Playbook.

This book will not transform you, but taking action on the steps certainly will.

The journey will change you, I promise.

If you know what you want (to build a coaching business) and you fully engage the challenge (work the plan in this book), you will experience the transformation you've been looking for. You will be a competent coach, a pillar in your community, a good friend to many, a terrific provider for you and your family, and, most importantly, a hero in an exciting story.

The question is not whether you have what it takes to build a great coaching business. The question is whether or not you will do the work to build a great coaching business.

Here's the great news: You are in complete control of the outcome.

Here's to your transformation.

■

To see sample websites, emails, and social media collateral that have worked to grow various coaching businesses or to join our coaching community, visit CoachBuilder.com. We would love to get to know you and to help you start, build, or scale your coaching business.

CoachBuilder.com

My team and I have built a special community at CoachBuilder.com.

Many people who are already coaches or who want to become coaches have valuable expertise but aren't sure how to leverage that expertise into a profitable coaching career. Sadly, many coaches quit on their dream of coaching because they've never been given the support and tools they need.

If you've been inspired by this book and want to follow through on the Coach Builder Playbook inside a community that will keep you motivated, consider joining the Coach Builder community.

Building a coaching career is not difficult. At Coach Builder, we've put together small groups complete with small group leaders to help you implement the Coach Builder Playbook so you are sure to follow through and succeed in your career. We have small groups for each of the three phases involved in building a coaching or consulting business: Build, Grow, and Scale.

The Coach Builder membership includes:

- An on-demand Coach Builder course that will help you build a profitable coaching business.

- Access to a dedicated coach whose sole objective is to get you past six figures in your coaching business.

- Small groups you can join so you can connect with other coaches and learn from their successes and failures.

- Exclusive livestreams covering a variety of topics that will help you build your coaching business.

- A product menu worksheet allowing you to brainstorm the products you will offer.

- Sample coaching websites you can see to inspire your own website.

- Sample lead generators you can either use or edit to build your own coaching business.

- Access to a plug-and-play CRM that includes preloaded emails you can start sending to potential clients immediately.

- Access to an email template allowing you to generate emails that close sales on your coaching products.

- A website wireframe tool allowing you to wireframe your coaching website to ensure it successfully converts to coaching sales.

- Access to on-demand coaching certifications in a wide range of topics so you can customize your certification and further equip yourself to get better results for your clients.

- Access to an annual Coach Builder Summit that will connect you to world-renowned thought leaders.

- A listing in our coaching directory at HireACoach.com.

Visit CoachBuilder.com and join the community today. How much faster could you build a profitable coaching career if you had a playbook and friends to help you work the plan?

Praise for the Coach Builder membership:

"When I decided to leave the comfort and stability of my position as the director of a nonprofit to launch my coaching business, I was full of excitement to help leaders learn from my past mistakes and successes. I was also filled with anxiety about what to charge, how to attract clients, and how to package coaching services that would create the desired results. Not only did the Coach Builder membership eliminate all those anxieties with insights and products, but it also opened up a community of coaches to glean insights from as I continue to build and refine my business going forward. Whether you feel insecure with your mindset or with the tangible tools to build a successful coaching business, Coach Builder has been the resource to create confidence that is so desperately needed to get your business off the runway and up to an altitude to soar."

—SETH WINTERHALTER,
business coach since 2022

"Before being part of the Coach Builder community I felt like I was alone on an island. When you're spending a majority of your time sharing your expertise with others, it's really important to replenish your reserves. The Coach Builder community is my wellspring! I lean into this community to satisfy my desire for continuous learning—sharpening the saw, as they say. It is also an amazing group of generous networkers who stand at the ready to share their perspective, give support, and cheer you on when you need a little inspiration. The Coach Builder community has become my extended family that I wouldn't want to live without!"

—SUSAN TRUMPLER,
business coach since 2013

"If those of us who are coaches share only one thing in common, it is that we are in the relationship business. And while there are a number of reasons I value being part of the Coach Builder community, the bottom line is that Coach Builder provides connections to a group of individuals that share my aspirations . . . are familiar with (and sharing ways to deal with) the same challenges and opportunities I wrestle with. Whether it is an arsenal of tools, practical counsel and coaching, or brainstorming a solution with a colleague, the entire community has a bias for supporting, assisting, innovating, and sharing anything that will help coaches serve clients and grow a vibrant business."

—ERIC FLETCHER,
business coach since 2017

Acknowledgments

A special thank you to my team: Tyler Ginn, Kyle Reid, Dr. JJ Peterson, Chad Cannon, Marlee Joseph, Andy Harrison, Aaron Alfrey, Bobby Richards, Dagne Harris, Sam Buchholz, Aundrea De Leon, Kari Loncar, Amy Smith, Macy Robison, Hilary Smith, Kelley Kirker, Prentice Sims, Tyler Bridges, Hannah Hitchcox, Suzanne Kelly, Paige McQueen, Lucas Alley, Esty Pittman, James Sweeting, Kyle Reed, Zach Grusznski, Josh Landrum, Aaron Alba, James Mitchell, and Jordan Tatro. And a very special thank you to Emily Pastina, who manages all our projects and tells me every morning what I am supposed to be working on. She frees me up to be creative, and I am grateful. Thanks as well to the hundreds of Business Made Simple Certified Coaches and StoryBrand Certified Guides who partner with us to help small business owners grow their businesses. Thanks also to our facilitators, who are constantly on the road presenting workshops on our sales and marketing frameworks.

A special thanks to Carey Murdock, who has kept me incredibly organized over the year it took for me to write this book.

I am also grateful for the long friendship and business relationships I've had with my agent and publisher. Wes Yoder is the world's best literary agent and has helped me dream up this book from day one. Thank you to Don Jacobson, Matt Baugher, and Mark Schoenwald.

As always, I'd be lost without my wife and purposeless without my daughter, Emmeline, plus our newest addition, Gloria (my wife's baby sister has moved in), with whom I get to dream about all things business and life.

Lastly, thank you. Thanks for believing in yourself and your coaching. I really believe coaches create winners, and we definitely need more stories about victories. Much love.

Index

About the Author

Donald Miller is the CEO of StoryBrand and Business Made Simple. He is the host of the Coach Builder YouTube Channel and is the author of several books, including bestsellers *Building a StoryBrand*, *Marketing Made Simple*, and *How to Grow Your Small Business*. He lives in Nashville, Tennessee, with his wife, Elizabeth, and their daughter, Emmeline.